Magnificent Kids!

Magnificent
Books

Reviews

"The world needs this book. It's not just a dose of inspiration; *Magnificent Kids!* brims and bursts with inspiration, hope, boldness and a clear way forward. If we're to turn the predicament of this planet around, we need more magnificent kids like those you'll meet within these pages. I'm so moved by them all. Heroes come in all shapes and sizes and here, you'll meet 23 of them who will move you to action, to be part of the change for a better society. Congratulations to all who worked on this fine and valuable project."
- ***Jo-Anne McArthur,***
Photographer and Author, "We Animals", and the 'We Animals Humane Education Programs'

"The difference one person can make has the potential to be hugely profound. *Magnificent Kids!* proves this over and over again. So many fantastic examples of small acts creating massive results."
- ***Janet Bray Attwood,***
NY Times Bestselling Author of "The Passion Test"

"With the utmost confidence, I know that *Magnificent Kids!* will not only inspire communities near and far, but will also help us to rediscover and redefine the real essence of all humanity - all seen and expressed through the simplistic eyes of an insightful child - simply brilliant!"
- ***Scott Katsura,***
International Recording Artist & Author of "I'm Writing My Own Story – A Kid's Guide To Becoming An Extraordinary Person"

"*Magnificent Kids!* shows that by encouraging a child's special interest, they can accomplish some wonderful achievements. I like the emphasis on what the child can do instead of dwelling on the deficits."
- ***Temple Grandin,***
Author of "The Autistic Brain" & "Thinking in Pictures"

"Anything is possible when we understand our own unique point of inspiration. *Magnificent Kids!* is a wonderful collection of inspiring stories from amazing and yet "every day" kids, who simply believe - they believe in their vision, they believe in their legacy and importantly, they believe in their capacity to change the world. In this way, they have tapped into their INSPIRATION and demonstrated what's possible. Read on...and be inspired!"
- **Heather Yelland,**
Director - Green SuperCamp International

"The young people showcased in *Magnificent Kids!* are indeed the leaders of tomorrow. This book clearly shows how everybody has the capacity to make a difference in this world."
- **Keith Leon,**
Multiple Bestselling Author, Book Publisher & Book Mentor

"*Magnificent Kids!* shows us why self-esteem is one of the key ingredients to success. These kids have found their passion and risen to great heights because they 'like' themselves and believe in their abilities. This book proves that anybody can do great things and that little steps build amazing outcomes."
- **Dr. Joe Rubino,**
Creator, www.HighSelfEsteemKids.com
& www.TheSelfEsteemBook.com
CEO, www.CenterForPersonalReinvention.com

"From humanity and animal welfare through to environmental issues, young people have their finger on the pulse. *Magnificent Kids!* brilliantly shows how anybody can tackle these issues simply by following their passions. This book is one step closer to a kinder world."
- **Helen Marston,**
Author of "Leo Escapes From The Lab" & CEO 'Humane Research Australia'

"Kerryn offers the world a true example of an individual who holds the planet and its blessings close to her heart. She gives all who have the pleasure of meeting her, an opportunity to shine with respect, love and kindness, and has an amazing ability to captivate and inspire all. Kerryn has managed to capture the true essence of her heart and what she holds dear within the pages of this remarkable book. *Magnificent Kids!* provides a wonderful opportunity to guide our children and ourselves into a world that is available to all of us, by opening our eyes to what we are all capable of achieving, with the tools, love and inspiration to guide us."

*- **Kristy Waddell,***
Director & Co-Founder - Planet Perspective Events

Magnificent Kids!

23 Superheroes
who are changing the world
- now it's your turn

The planet is waiting for you!

Kerryn Vaughan

Magnificent
Books

DISCLAIMER:
This information and material contained within this publication has been written and published solely for educational and inspirational purposes and is not meant for individual advice. Should any reader choose to make use of the information contained herein, this is their decision and the contributors (and their companies/organisations), author and publishers shall have neither liability nor responsibility to any person or entity with respect to any loss, damage or injury caused or alleged to be caused directly or indirectly by the information contained in the book. It is recommended that the reader obtain their own independent advice.

First Edition 2014

10 9 8 7 6 5 4 3 2 1

Copyright © 2014 Kerryn Vaughan

All rights reserved. No part of this book may be reproduced or transmitted in any form or by any means whatsoever without written permission from the author, except for brief quotations used for reviews.

Cover photo: Avalon Theisen © Conserve It Forward Inc.

Cover Design: James William - New York / USA

National Library of Australia Cataloguing-in-Publication entry:

Vaughan, Kerryn, 1963 -
 Magnificent Kids!: 23 Superheroes who are changing the world - now it's your turn / Kerryn Vaughan

   ISBN   978-0-9924275-0-4 (paperback).

     1.Role models - Juvenile literature. 2. Conduct of life - Juvenile literature. 3. Children - Attitudes - Juvenile literature. 4. Attitude change in children. 5. Self-confidence. I Title

305.2355

Printed in the USA

To all the amazing kids out there who have
not yet realised their magnificence.
May this book be the inspiration
for finding your hidden Superhero!

To my sister Carolyn.
I will always love your magnificent kids
as though they were mine.
I wish you were here to see this.

"If we are to teach real peace in this world,
and if we are to carry on a real war against war,
we shall have to begin with the children."
~ Mohandas Ghandi

Acknowledgements

First and foremost, I would like to extend my deepest and most sincere gratitude and love to my parents and sisters. While I have protested about almost everything from the day I was born, your love and support have not once quavered through my tantrums and the plethora of twists and turns that have determined my life journey. Thank you.

To my dear friend Kristy Waddell for offering your shoulder day after day, night after night, and continuing to guide me through my tormented wish to leave a legacy so that this world might just be a better place because I was in it.

To my dear friend Maggie Griffin for editing and proof reading this book and somehow managing to negotiate the interwoven complexities of the grammatical rules of Australian and American English. Your generosity and perseverance are greatly appreciated; your job can't have been easy on my expressive days!

To my 'Braddah' Scott Katsura - Mahalo nui loa for believing in me every step of the way, and for offering endless support and the warmest Aloha spirit.

To the very talented David Simpson for the amazing sketches. I still don't know how you do that!

To the incredible James William for the brilliant cover design.

To the countless people who have buzzed in and out of my life over the past decades. You thought you were learning from me, but you have been my greatest teachers. This book happened in honour of your magnificence.

And last but by no means least, every magnificent kid who has contributed their story to this book. It would not have happened without you and for that I can not thank you all enough. You are the shining stars of today, and the leaders of tomorrow!

XII

Contents

Introduction 1
1. Alec Urbach 5
2. Alyssa Deraco 17
3. Avalon Theisen 25
4. Carter and Olivia Ries 39
5. Clover Hogan 53
6. Dallas Jessup 61
7. Dani Bowman 75
8. Daniel and William Clarke 89
9. Jack Andraka 105
10. Jessica Carscadden 113
11. Jordyn Schara 121
12. Liva Adelstorp 137
13. Louis Robinson 145
14. Luca Berardi 153
15. Max Wallack 161
16. Nicholas Lowinger 175
17. Olivia Bouler 187
18. Olivia Wright 195
19. Samuel Lam 203
20. Shekhar Kumar 215
21. Toby King 227
Author's Final Word 235
Special Note to Parents and Teachers 237
What's Your Cause? 255

"Children are unique and perfect
representations of themselves.
They are not miniature versions of us waiting to
grow up with the same ideals and beliefs.
They are magnificent individuals,
who when given every opportunity to
express their own interests,
values and authenticity without judgement,
have the capacity to change the world."
~ Kerryn Vaughan

Foreword

Magnificent Kids! - it is more than just a book about 23 extraordinary kids who are leading by example. It is a book about continual empowerment, and how role models do positively impact future generations. While there are many books out there that are compilations of stories, what stood out for me in *Magnificent Kids!* was one key word – "passion". Yes, the passion that the author, Kerryn Vaughan has shown while putting this book together, and the passion that is so evident in the stellar efforts of the 'superhero' in each story.

Many years ago, I had the honour and the privilege of meeting Kerryn. Besides her contagious smile, her passion was something that stood out for me upon meeting her for the first time.

Having worked with young people myself, I realise the need for books such as these. Books that will give children hope, hope that will allow them to recognise their potential, potential that will make them role models.

This book is full of role models who are leaving behind a trail of inspiration. Each story carries a unique message. The common thread that links each unique message is that children can rise despite obstacles in their path. You will find that the person in each story did extraordinary things, and not necessarily because they believed that they were extraordinary. They did it because they allowed their passion to drive them forward, and their persistence in the pursuit of creating a better world paid off in the end.

Many of the stories in this book clearly show that if you are willing to do the best that you can, with the best that you have, then you are a winner! A winning attitude is so apparent in most of the stories you will read in this book. That winning attitude is carried by the author in her quest to empower kids all over the globe.

So, if you are a parent, a teacher, a sports coach for kids, if you work with kids with disabilities, or are involved with kids in any other capacity, I strongly suggest that you share this book with kids. Enlighten them with the gems of wisdom contained in each chapter. Let them know that their passions are worth pursuing, and their goals can become a reality if they persist.

My belief is that every single child in the world has the ability to create something magnificent, leave a legacy behind, and be remembered for creating something magnificent. It is the role of adults to support children in creating and maintaining a self image that will allow them to create something significant. Kerryn has done an admirable job in doing just that.

This book should be available in every single school so that children can read or hear these inspiring stories, and say to the superheroes in this book, "If you can, I can".

As you pick up this book to read it, please remember one thing – you have in your hands, a collection of outstanding stories that can positively impact any child's life. Please make it your responsibility to share these stories. Pick up an extra copy for a child who will find tremendous value in these stories, and rise to their greatness. By helping others rise, you will rise yourself.

Thank you once again Kerryn for your dedication, passion and persistence in creating a better world for our future leaders (the children of today).

Ronny Prasad – *Author of WELCOME TO YOUR LIFE (simple insights for your inspiration and empowerment).*

Introduction

Magnificent:
'Grand or noble in thought or deed'
'Outstanding of its kind'

Congratulations! If you have this book in your hands, you are already a change maker. You know the world needs you and deep down you know you rock.

Magnificent Kids! features 23 superheroes who have chosen to use their skills, talents and passions to make a difference, and every one of them started their project when they were younger than 18 years of age. They share stories about themselves and provide answers to the questions we most want to ask incredible people. What you will find amazing is that the kids in this book are actually just like you.

They have all set up projects that help humanity, animals or the planet. You will be blown away at what they have achieved with very little other than their determination to succeed. They have been driven by their passion, utilised their skills and talents, asked for support, and have created magic.

What I really love about these stories is that some are really lengthy and have a lot of detail while others tell how it all works with very few words. I love that there is such variety. It absolutely represents how each person has their own unique style, and no matter what that style is, there is no right or wrong way to do anything and we all have a very valuable story.

Some people think you have to be the most intelligent kid in your grade to do amazing things. Not true! While some of the kids in this book are incredibly academic, it's not necessarily the main driver for success. In fact, all the kids share with you what they believe are the key ingredients for success. You will find that these are the very same ingredients you have in your own pantry of life.

Other people think you have to be really rich to change the world but that is also incorrect. These guys have done awesome things with very little money. You can read their answers about financial assistance and some of them even used the money from their own piggy banks to get started. Some have travelled the world and visited some amazing places, and that is purely because they were driven and passionate enough to raise the funds to follow their dreams. But we don't need to travel the globe to make a difference. The crayfish in the local restaurant would love you to set her free. The elderly lady down the road will live a happier life if you smile and chat with her when you pass by. The dog rescue centre in the next town will really appreciate your help every week, and your school might love to run a recycling program. You can even get your friends to help you raise funds for clean water wells in Africa. There is always an easy, inexpensive and local way to make a profound difference.

So if these projects are not necessarily driven by being very rich or very smart, what does drive them? Passion! What is obvious, is that you need to know what you are passionate about. What is that thing you really love or feel very strongly about? If you're not sure about what your passion is or what really drives you to make change, check out the 'What's your cause?' section at the back of this book. If you are passionate about something, you will have an abundance of energy to put into it and you are more likely to succeed and stay focused.

Your generation has the courage, determination, creativity, and curiosity to fearlessly ask, 'Why is this happening, and how can I fix it?' There is a sense of responsibility and purpose unique to young people of today. You do not see any issue as too big, and you never shy away from presenting 'out of the box' solutions.

I feel privileged to produce something special that will help create change in the way young people think and feel about themselves. I want to show you that anybody can achieve great things, and that every single person has incredible magnificence within them, just waiting to be unlocked.

Magnificent Kids!

I invited these 23 incredible young people to join me on this journey, to show just how amazing it feels to be aligned with your passions and authenticity, knowing that every little thing you do creates a huge ripple effect in this world. As you share their journeys, you will begin to see that you too have just what it takes to make a difference. Each of these stories is as remarkable as the next and because there was no way I could determine an order of preference, you will see that they are in alphabetical order according to their first name. From the bottom of my heart I thank each and every one of these superheroes for their contribution to this book and to the planet, and I thank you for believing in yourself.

I just can't wait to see how much better the world becomes as a result of your being inspired by their stories, and starting up your own magnificent projects.

I believe that every single person is magnificent, and I believe in you! So get your superhero outfit on and show the world what you are truly made of.

"We all have the capacity to be a superhero.
In order to become one, you just have to
find your unique power or ability
and exploit it for the greater good.
The cape and mask are optional accessories,
but a kind heart is essential."
~ Robert Clancy

Alec Urbach

There are no heroics involved in making creative, consistent social change. It is my belief that to create a more peaceful, humane society, we must aim for an educated and intellectually hungry society - and we begin by empowering children. After meeting clergy-educators from Ghana at a benefit concert for international healthcare, and watching footage reporting the unacceptably dire state of healthcare and education in Ghana's poorest villages, I wanted to use my talents to help. At first I thought, *"There is no way I can fix this. There's just too much suffering; too much illiteracy."* I wasn't sure how my talents or skills could benefit the lives of millions of disenfranchised kids. After all, I was here in America, safe and healthy, and all I had were my passion and ideals.

Then a light went on. I remembered a quote by Elie Wiesel, *"Silence encourages the tormentor, never the tormented."* I wouldn't be silent. I would use my voice as a story-teller and filmmaker. I would create a paradigm shift in "developing nation education" through film and educational comic books. So I founded **'Giving from the Ground Up'** (and its subsidiary, **'Alec's Animated Schoolhouse'**) to produce elementary school science, math &

hygiene curricula for animation, along with companion educational comic books on social issues like bullying, staying in school and negative peer pressure. All of these created a cartoon animated "global classroom" that could overcome the literacy divide in developing nations by teaching **visually**.

With the collaboration of talented illustrators and language consultants to translate the learning modules and comic books into Spanish for Central and South America, *Alec's Animated Schoolhouse* is poised to expand its new curriculum worldwide to reach the world's most vulnerable children. Being a bit of an artistic rebel, I prefer breaking down obstacles rather than being deterred by them, and so my organization uses vibrant, colorful, lovable and funny cartoon-animated creatures to reach across the learning divide. The *Animated Schoolhouse* workbooks, videos and comics are jam-packed with characters and creatures like Hattie the Hummingbird, Phinnaeus F. Fox, Mr. Leibowitz and Miss Olive (the math and science teachers), a global-rock 'n' roll cartoon-animated band, "The Digits" (performing original songs on DVD to help teach each math lesson), and cartoon workbooks that rely on visual learning. By teaching the investigative process and scientific method via film and comics, whether in the absence of literacy or in the presence of learning challenges, one can be taught how to transform industry - from building windmills to testing the most drought-resistant crops. I am pleased to share photos of some of our students learning: http://tinyurl.com/2013Ghana .

In 2012, I was privileged to be selected as one of '*The 25 Most Powerful and Influential Young People*', and was awarded the Youth Service America Award; as well as the National Caring Award. I have been a keynote speaker at the Amnesty International Human Rights Conference, DC, and I have presented numerous TEDx talks. In 2012, I was also fortunate enough to be chosen as a torch bearer for the London Olympics (sponsored by Coca Cola). In 2013, I won the National AXA Achievement Scholarship Award for Academics and Leadership in the United States; and was selected for two of Princeton University's most sought after fellowships: '*The Princeton Entrepreneurship TigerTrek Fellowship/Trip to Silicon Valley;* and '*Inside Israel Diplomatic Fellowship*' with Ambassador Kurtzer. I have a deep interest in entrepreneurship (especially social enterprise) and a continuing fascination with government, diplomacy and conflict negotiation.

Now a freshman at Princeton University, I am thrilled to be assembling students from around the world to help translate and illustrate my educational comic books, and become part of this educational comic book revolution. Interested in education reform? Want to lend a hand? Contact me.

What does the word 'magnificent' mean to you?

It means unshakeable; positive; willing to fail in order to create something of merit.

What do you give to the world?

As a writer and dedicated student of education, I see that for each student who learns something the traditional way, there may be two who learn it differently. We understood this need to see things through cartoons, animal drawings, comics and comic videos when we were in nursery and kindergarten - so did our teachers and administrators. We didn't just hear about numbers, or see numbers on a textbook page or write numbers. We colored them, cut them out, built them and sang about them. Then it ended. But there are children who continue to learn best through **parts**: the visual, the auditory, the tactile… they need those other tools in order to get that equation; grasp the moral; infer from an experiment. We, as educational innovators and "serial deconstructors," need to provide those tools to help kids BECOME. Teach kids the **parts**… they'll create the **whole**.

I hope that my voice as a storyteller will create a paradigm shift in "developing nation education" through film and educational comic books - breaking down math and science; hygiene and social issues into accessible, bite-sized pieces - bridging the learning divide among the world's most vulnerable children.

Why is this important to you?

I wanted to express to young people in the arts and education that although it's comfortable working with a model we know (i.e. traditional education), if we hesitate to build the new, we stop thinking big, and then we stop **becoming**. We, as students, need to identify the pressing social issues upon which we can have an impact. Don't be afraid that someone has already done it or that someone can do it better. Your talent is unique. Your talent is special. So write a song, do a documentary, translate a lesson in your favorite subject into the multiple languages you know. Imagine the impact, the boundless leverage available to us, the elasticity of creation - once we begin to **deconstruct** traditional education and **become** builders of dreams and innovators of learning.

Why did you choose the project/idea that you did?

I chose my particular mode of global outreach because it utilized the skills I had and had nurtured. As a student at NY Film Academy and Long Island High School for the Arts during part of my day and weekend each week (as well as holding down a full AP course schedule in my public high school), I was surrounded by the world of film and creative writing. It made sense that the adventure of creating new avenues for education in developing nations through filmmaking and comic books would enable me to engage in a meaningful way as a citizen of the world. It is not the mere existence of each distinct community in our world that makes society diverse, but how these communities unite to work towards healing the world and making it a more peaceful and extraordinary place. I have worked and fundraised and used my talents to catalyze innovative educational ideas for the developing world since the age of 13; have been selected as one of 25 students internationally to be a Global Teen Leader for *Three Dot Dash* - attending the week-long *International Peace Summit in NYC* as a representative of the United States; and I have donated my filmmaking abilities to young, ground-breaking charitable organizations in developing nations that need Public Service Announcements (PSA's) and more public attention for their missions. Often it is the groups with which we surround ourselves that propel us forward to our goals.

How old were you when you began your project?

13 years old.

How did you go about getting it started?

After meeting clergy from Ghana at a benefit concert for international healthcare at Lincoln Center, and watching footage reporting the dire state of healthcare and education in their poorest villages, I wanted to use my talents to help. At first I thought, "There is no way I can fix this. There's just too much suffering; too much illiteracy." I wasn't sure how my talents as a film maker and writer could affect the lives of millions of disenfranchised kids. After all, I was here in America, safe and healthy, and all I had were my passion and ideals. But, I realized that although I couldn't save children whose lives had already been ravaged by poverty and a lack of education, - I *could* change many others. I could create unique scripts for lessons in math, science and healthcare to be animated for use in schools worldwide with access to even one computer - because visual lessons disarm the vulnerable learner and help the material cross the literacy barrier - what could be better for a child with low motivation to attend school, than watching colourful, funny and cheeky characters teaching the most difficult subjects to learn - math and science! I could create socially conscious comic books with colorful, comical characters to teach ethics while circumventing the learning divide; I could use my organizational and leadership skills to rally kids across the country to collect school supplies and send them, through my organization, to Ghanaian villages. I had to use my gifts as a story-teller and entrepreneur. I could not be complacent.

Who is your project benefiting, and how?

At present, the nations using our books and video lessons are in Africa, South America, and the United States. We have Spanish translations, and just finished our Arabic translations of the comic books, and will be starting the Hebrew, Farsi and French versions next month. I do hope that the socially conscious comic books catch on in Australian and European schools as well.

Who were the key people that supported you, and how?

My parents always had positive responses to my desire to use my writing skills and my mind for social good and this made me believe that I could create work that mattered. When one's parents are behind them, a young person feels empowered. Additionally, it was organizations like *Nestle Very Best in Youth* and *Three Dot Dash/We Are Family Foundation* that initially believed in my work and the positive creative changes it would make in developing world education. They supported me through small grants and connection to mentors. *Three Dot Dash* is especially efficient as an organization because the founders and mentors stay in touch with you for at least a year after you've been chosen as a Global Teen Leader. They have networking events each year, enabling their Global Teen Leaders to continue making connections that will be valuable for a lifetime.

How much financial assistance did you have, and from whom?

I wrote grants constantly and applied to organizations for scholarships based on leadership. Nestle, Three Dot Dash and NSHSS (National Society of HS Scholars - led by Claes Nobel of the Nobel Prize Family) were always supportive.

How will you keep your project going into the future?

It is extraordinarily difficult to keep a non-profit moving forward without always asking for money or writing for grants - especially when a young person is trying to bootstrap the organization from scratch. Therefore, I have founded a social enterprise: *'Worldwise Comics'* - a for-profit that has a "social good" component. In this way, I can send both my books and donations from my company's profits to schools in need around the world. I think we all should start thinking in terms of social businesses as the way of the future if we wish to be successful in making global changes.

How have your peers responded to you setting up the project, and do they (or can they) get involved in any way?

I found that my peers in high school were not as interested in public service or global outreach. Of course, this is understandable because leadership is thought about as school club-based in most academic environments; and at top public schools, any spare time is spent prepping for class and standardized exams. It's just the nature of our overly exam-focused environment. When I joined with other young social entrepreneurs at conferences or organization meetings from those groups that sponsor young global leaders, our discussions revolved around how we could work with each other or move our own work forward in positive ways. At Princeton University, I have met throngs of young people who are interested in, enthusiastic about, and already working towards their own public service projects and social enterprises. This generation is serious about its hunger for making positive change globally.

Do you see yourself as ordinary or extraordinary?

This question disturbs me. Clearly if a young person pushes boundaries and creates anything above marginal success in their chosen field, or in a personal project under their own steam, they are deeply devoted individuals. Yet why would we call such a person extraordinary. Einstein was extraordinary. Itzhak Perlman is extraordinary. Jobs, Gates and Musk are extraordinary. We use that term too easily in common parlance. So, as to how I see myself: certainly extraordinary is not a word I would choose. I am passionate about my studies and projects; I am a mover; I am not afraid to fail, nor am I afraid to dream. I am a self-motivated, hard worker who loves to learn for the sake of learning, and I expect to be engaged in that process for a lifetime. I am someone who would like to leave the world a little better for having been here. What I think is that having the chance to "learn" is extraordinary. If I can take my personal spin on learning things that others haven't assimilated, and then teach those things to help build my own company - I will have done something meaningful, exciting and helpful on a grand scale.

What is the most important thing to you?

Finding that one thing in life at any given time that means the most to me, and having the strength, foresight and creativity to follow it, feed it and make a success out of it.

What are your strengths?

Creativity; Communication; Public Speaking; Marketing and Social Media skill; Entrepreneurial personality - a "thoughtful" risk taker; Positive Attitude; Brain Storming; Self-Motivation (I'm a self-studier, so if I want to learn about something to improve my organization or business, I study everything I can get my hands on).

What are your weaknesses?

I don't like saying NO to people. I also wish I had the temperament for coding!

Does your project require you to focus on your strengths?

Yes; but it also requires me to be an aggressive prospector for the best talent in the fields of arts and coding. I've learned that the successful scope of a project often depends on the collaborative efforts of a number of talents.

Who is your greatest role model and why?

My brother founded the international musical non-profit, *Children Helping Children/Concerts for a Cure* when he was 9 years old. He was one of the earliest "child social entrepreneurs" in the nation. A Juilliard prodigy, he raised over $5 million for pediatric neurological research and hospital programs by travelling the country performing Benefit Concerts in esteemed halls like: Carnegie Hall, Lincoln Center and their national peers in major cities. He won the *World of Children Award* for Global Child Advocacy, and then the *National Jefferson Award for Public Service* (founded by Jacqueline Kennedy Onassis and Sam Beard), our country's Nobel Prize for Public Service, and then stepped into the position of National Director of the Jefferson Awards.

Of all the people in the world, who inspires you the most?

My mother - an endless, loving, positive-spirited support.

How/where/why did you learn to care globally?

I learned to care globally by growing up in my family with the concept of Tsedakah (Charity). I was taught that we all have a part in healing the world. We just have to figure out what our individual role will be.

If you could change one thing in the world, what would it be?

The way religion informs the way we look at and behave towards each other.

What do you think are the ingredients for success?

You have to be hungry to be successful. My brother taught me that. Hunger and belief in the project you are creating are the first steps to success. Then, it's all about networking and transferring your excitement and interest to the people who can help you to move your work forward.

What is your global vision?

My global vision is the empowerment of my generation and the next through education, global youth counsels and youth diplomatic missions, to create a dialogue that is polite, open, honest and accepting. All we have now is a dialogue of finger pointing and posturing. We have begun the hard work in my generation thanks to a number of socially conscious organizations for youth, but we have a tough road ahead to make the aforementioned environment a reality.

What would be your message to the world?

Use your power and transfer your passion to whomever you meet. Passion is contagious and so is creativity. Creativity needs to be practiced every day so that it becomes part of your muscle memory - as essential to you as breathing. Only with creativity can we be truly innovative.

If other kids wanted to start up their own magnificent project, what advice would you give them and what steps would you suggest they take?

Start building your project under your own steam; take advice from others who have built non-profit organizations and succeeded, but then do things your way and follow your heart. Do not become a puppet for a Board of Directors. Do not let yourself become a figurehead. After spending time really talking with the best of these young, smart leaders, it's easy to tell who has the real goods. There are many great, articulate, smart young people from all over the world creating life-changing programs in their nations. Imagine connecting and collaborating to make each other's projects even more universalistic and positive. So, attend as many TEDx events and social good conferences as you can; speak to the presenters; share your ideas. The chances are that someone will know a "game-changer" who can help take your plan to a new stage. Remember, use your power!

http://fromgroundup.org

"We worry about what a child will become tomorrow, yet we forget that he is someone today."
~ Stacia Tauscher

Alyssa Deraco

Every holiday season as we get wrapped up in making sure everyone has the perfect gift(s), making sure our Christmas trees have the correct number of ornaments and our homes have just enough flashing lights, there will be many children not fortunate enough to experience this excitement and the excesses of the festive season. Some of these kids don't have a home, new clothes or all the other luxuries that so many of us take for granted every day.

Hi, my name is Alyssa Deraco and I'm 15 years old. I live in Lancaster, Pennsylvania and I'm in 10th grade. I enjoy cats, dogs, playing soccer, singing, swimming and of course, reading. I enjoy helping others and I wanted to give kids who don't have much, a way of forgetting their troubles by reading. Books have helped me through the divorce of my parents and I want to share my love of books and reading with kids to help them too. My grandmother always wanted me to read, so I read a lot with her.

My parents always taught me to give and not to take things for granted, and because of the love and encouragement of my family and friends, I have been able to make my dream come alive. My

Magnificent Kids!

Mom grew up in poverty in Guatemala and felt very blessed when she was adopted at 12 years of age by a family in Lancaster. Mom never forgot how hard her childhood was and always wanted me to know that there are a lot of people who really struggle. She used to take me into Lancaster to show me the homeless shelter and the rescue mission. I really felt the message Mom was giving me and I really wanted to do something.

Five years ago, when I was 10 years old, I started collecting books and pajamas to give to kids of all ages because I wanted to make a difference in their lives. In 2008 my Mom and I started a Non-profit charity called ***Alyssa's Bedtime Stories***. We started out collecting used books and then new books and then it grew to pajamas and it just keeps growing and growing. Five of my friends are now part of my team as it's becoming too much for just Mom and me. Our purpose is to donate gifts of new books and pajamas to children in need, during the Christmas and Hanukkah season. We are dedicated to giving hope to children through a simple act of kindness and generosity. ***Alyssa's Bedtime Stories*** won the Red Rose Award in 2011 for encouraging children to read.

We've donated thousands of children's books and pajamas to Lancaster area organizations such as Milagro house, Clare house, domestic violence services of Lancaster and many more. Every package that ***Alyssa's Bedtime Stories*** sends out is labelled by name, if possible, and then hand-delivered. The entire process is very personalized. So far we have donated more than 10,000 packages of books and 5,000 packages of pajamas, and includes deliveries to many underprivileged children in Guatemala, Ecuador, and Honduras.

Every year just before Christmas, we hold a fundraising event to help support our cause. We choose this time of year because it allows us to buy books and pajamas so they can be given to the children as holiday gifts just in time for Christmas. This past Christmas alone, the group was able to create and distribute about 900 packages of books and pajamas.

One day, during the early years, Mom and I were arguing and it was really bad. We had to drop off a donation so we went to Milagro House and we saw the kids and very quickly realized that they were doing it tough. Right after that, we were fine and happy and hugged each other. We were arguing about something so dumb and it kind of brings us back to the realization that we've come a long way and we're at a very good place. It's great because I get to see how happy the kids are when they receive their gifts and it constantly makes me appreciate what I have and I also know that I'm making a difference in this world.

What does the word 'magnificent' mean to you?

Something or an act that makes you say "wow". It takes your breath away.

What do you give to the world?

I feel that I may not give too much to the world, but with my charity and a warm smile, I've changed lives.

Why is this important to you?

Alyssa's Bedtime Stories is the world to me. It has definitely opened my eyes to things I would never have seen or even known about and it has given me many amazing opportunities.

Why did you choose the project/idea that you did?

Books have always been my 'best friends' through the hardships that I've faced in my life. As for the pajamas, who wouldn't want to cuddle up in a warm pair of pajamas and indulge themselves with a good book?

How old were you when you began your project?

I was 10yrs old.

How did you go about getting it started?

I introduced the idea to my Mom and it took off from there.

Who is your project benefiting, and how?

Mostly children, but it also gives parents a way to bond with their children at bedtime.

Who were the key people that supported you, and how?

My parents have always supported my dreams and helped me make them come true.

How much financial assistance did you have, and from whom?

A lot!!! A charity is not cheap or easy and we couldn't do it without the help from friends, family and local businesses.

How will you keep your project going into the future?

It is something I'm passionate about and always will be. Maybe it will allow us to go to other countries like Guatemala. Who knows? My project has taken me so very far in the last five years. We have met so many interesting people, who we would never have met without the charity.

How have your peers responded to you setting up the project, and do they (or can they) get involved in any way?

Everyone seems to have a good response to what we're doing and think it's pretty cool. Yes we have ways for people to get involved but donating and volunteering their time to drop off packages are the best ways to help.

Do you see yourself as ordinary or extraordinary?

I see myself as both. I'm an ordinary girl with an extraordinary dream and a love for helping others.

What is the most important thing to you?

My family. They've always been on my side through everything and have never ever let me down.

What are your strengths?

Working hard and doing things the best I can!

What are your weaknesses?

I'm a little disorganized.

Does your project require you to focus on your strengths?

Yes! Because every package has to be done correctly. We want every kid to know we did it with care and love.

Who is your greatest role model and why?

My Mom is my greatest role model. She has flaws like everyone else but she's beautiful and confident.

Of all the people in the world, who inspires you the most?

All of the other charity owners. It takes commitment and hard work to run a charity.

How/where/why did you learn to care globally?

I was brought up to give. The best feeling is giving, especially when you can see the faces of the kids light up by giving a simple gift. My Mom was born in Guatemala and lived there until she was 12. She shares many stories of how she grew up in poverty and how hard life was. She had nothing when she was a kid and struggled every day to make ends meet. That's why it is important for us to give to kids in Guatemala and other countries too.

If you could change one thing in the world, what would it be?

How much sadness and hate a lot of people hold inside. It weighs people down like a brick in water.

What do you think are the ingredients for success?

Never giving up! Do your best at all times.

What is your global vision?

To help as many kids as possible, not only in our community but around the world.

What would be your message to the world?

You can do anything. Don't ever let anyone dull your sparkle.

If other kids wanted to start up their own magnificent project, what advice would you give them and what steps would you suggest they take?

Research where the need is, who can help you, what you can do to help others and are you willing to make the time for it?

www.alyssasbedtimestories.org

"I continue to believe that if children are given the necessary tools to succeed, they will succeed beyond their wildest dreams."
~ David Vitter

Avalon Theisen

My name is Avalon Theisen. I am 13 years old and I live in Tampa, Florida, USA. I was born in Richmond, Virginia but I have lived in Tampa since I was a few months old. I love swimming, reading interesting books, being with my friends, horses and art. I also like watching documentaries and playing board games. I really love being outdoors in nature, and always have, even as a baby. I have a beautiful mother and a great father. My siblings are 3 dogs, Kumba, Angel and Max. I love them very much and at least one of them is with me every second I am at home. We live on a small lake, so lots of animals end up in our house, whether it is on purpose or by accident.

When I was 8, I started taking herpetology classes with Mr. George L. Heinrich of Heinrich Ecological Services. I am home-schooled, so that means my education is based out of my home, but my classes are everywhere on Earth. If I could, I would take a class on a different planet, too! I also started going to frog listening workshops and learning to be a citizen scientist who identifies frogs by their sounds and reports on them. I have learned that frogs are an important indicator species. If an area has lots of native frogs, then it is probably healthy. But if the native frogs are disappearing or dying out, then there is a problem. Unfortunately, frogs are disappearing world-wide.

I already had a connection with the natural world, but this information inspired me with an idea of how I could help people connect more effectively with the environment. After taking citizen science classes at Camp Bayou Outdoor Learning Center when I was 9 years old, I was given the chance to pick my favorite topic to share with people at an event. Of course, I chose frogs. Frogs are everywhere in the world, except for Antarctica, and even when you cannot see them, you can hear them. There are lots of small ways for people to help frogs and when we help frogs, we are helping the environment.

I kept going to frog listening workshops, and taking herpetology, conservation, and nature classes. I still do all of these things and continue to learn skills which help me to share information with others. After I had my first frog booth, I was invited to a school to give my first PowerPoint presentations. Since then, I have shared information and ideas to help thousands of people, through my interactive booths, presentations, listening hikes and events. With the help of many volunteers, I planned and ran Save the Frogs Day events in 2011, 2012 and 2013 in the Tampa, Florida area. Save the Frogs Day is an international day of amphibian conservation and awareness and was started by the organization SAVE THE FROGS! It is held on the last Friday of every April. Events are independently planned worldwide. In 2010, I wrote a speech about Save the Frogs Day to share with my nature class.

I also started communicating more with Dr. Kerry Kriger, the founder of SAVE THE FROGS! The organization has taught me many things and has been very supportive and helpful; especially during my first year. I wanted the Tampa Bay area to have a Save The Frogs Day event as we have so many amphibians in Florida and our environment is so much a part of what our city and state are about. I decided to plan a Save the Frogs Day event for 2011. In 2011, 2012 and 2013, I planned and ran the Tampa Bay area Save the Frogs Day events at a local nature preserve called Camp Bayou Outdoor Learning Center. This Center has supported my efforts since I began. We had games, activities, prizes and education all about saving frogs and other amphibians. I also delivered presentations and led frog listening hikes. Our events are free and full of froggy fun for families! I hope that after the events, people are empowered with new information and ways to act and that they feel more connected with the natural world. At some point, my project became known as **Conserve It Forward** and it is still known by that name even though it is a 501(c)3 federal non-profit organization. Amphibian conservation, specifically frogs, is still the main focus of what I do, but as my organization has grown, so have the topics that we spread awareness for.

I am honored to have been invited to speak at many events that include:

- TEDxYouth Tampa Bay, Florida (2013)
- Save the Frogs Day (2011, 2012, 2013)
- Downtown Atlanta Earth Cleanup Challenge Celebration (2012)
- Green Trends Conference - opening presenter, Florida (2012)
- Party for Planet Earth Day (2011, 2012)
- Action for Nature International Eco Hero reception, San Francisco (2012)

At TEDxYouth Tampa Bay (Nov 2013), I presented my story about how I started doing what I do and my presentation included information about amphibian conservation. The theme of the 2013 TEDxYouthDay was "The Spark" and how you will spark change. My presentation "How the Croak of the Wild Empowered the Child" focused on what sparked me into getting involved in amphibian conservation, and also how I now spark others to make a positive change.

I am very happy and proud to be a recipient of the 2012 Temple Grandin Award. This award is sponsored by Future Horizons Inc. and is given to people with autism or Asperger's Syndrome who have achieved major endeavors. I have met Dr. Temple Grandin twice, once in San Francisco and once in Miami. She is amazing, very intelligent and I love her stories. She is also very inspirational!

Magnificent Kids!

In 2012, a mutual friend in the conservation world, introduced **Conserve It Forward** to Pacha's Pajamas and Balance Edutainment. We kept in touch, and when they were preparing for their new CD, they asked if I would like to help bring amphibians to it. Of course, I said yes! I am very happy to be the voice of Abbey Toad featured on 'Pacha's Pajamas: A Story Written by Nature, Vol. 2,' track 20. "Pacha's Pajamas" is a children's pop musical that inspires youth and families to be superheroes for the planet.

I am a spokesperson for Heal Our World, Heal Ourselves. This campaign is about positive and healthy entertainment, and asks mass media to offer more programming and media for children and their families that do 3 things:
1) highlight the good things going on in the world,
2) inspire kids to use their creativity and take positive actions, and
3) encourage entertainment that changes how kids and their families see the world!

Kids spend a lot of time in front of screens, so if what they were seeing was more positive and empowering, then they would be more inspired to do great things for themselves and the world.

Many schools, when teaching science classes, will have students dissect real frogs. Many thousands of frogs die from this each year. Using real frogs is expensive because you have to pay for frogs and all the equipment. It smells very bad and can be messy. Kids do not need this kind of experience. Plus, killing all of those frogs is just wrong. Obviously you cannot re-use them for future dissections, either.

I prepared a video titled "Effectiveness of Digital Frog Dissection Software" to promote digital dissection as an alternative to using real frogs. After seeing my video, Froguts Inc. rewarded me by donating software for prizes at my 2011, 2012 and 2013 Tampa Bay area Save the Frogs events. Digital Frog, another company, offers a software discount code for my **Conserve It Forward** followers and has also helped me put together educator packs.

With digital dissections or dissection software, you can get a license for home or school use, and you can use the same frogs over and over. If you need help on a certain body system, you can re-do that part of the software. For schools, dissection software is much cheaper, and students won't be upset about smell and cutting open a real frog. Digital dissection is the best kind of dissection for everyone, if you want to learn about anatomy and body systems.

Recently, **Conserve It Forward** joined the world's largest partnership for amphibian conservation, the Amphibian Survival Alliance. I am currently working with the editors of FrogLog, an amphibian conservation publication, to create FrogLog Jr which will be aimed at school aged children. FrogLog Jr will include positive amphibian conservation stories, fun amphibian facts, activities for kids and students, conservationist profiles, ways you can take action and so much more! More information can be found at http://www.amphibians.org/froglog.

I have always wanted a television show about nature, so I can reach a bigger audience. In summer 2013, I submitted a show proposal to The Autism Channel which airs on streaming television. They liked my idea and the show is called *"Nature Tracks With Avalon"*. I have been filming for several months now and my show started airing late 2013. Since it is streaming television, you can watch whenever you want and don't have to wait for re-runs. Also, people can watch from anywhere in the world.

One exciting thing that happened at the end of 2013 was that Youth Leader Magazine included frogs and me in their new inspirational Change Generation Rising Card Game & Multimedia Action Pack! It was an honor to be part of this project, along with many other friends and youth from around the world.

In 2013 I was also invited to be a founding member of the International A-Team for Wildlife, a group of conservation prodigies and environmental youth leaders from around the world, all working together for endangered species.

Recently I received the 2014 WEDU Be More Inspiring Rising Star Award. This award recognizes individuals under 21 years of age who have distinguished themselves in the community directly accredited to their inspiration, dedication, motivation or acts of kindness. Other awards I have received, which include international awards, are the Roosevelt-Ashe Conservation Award for Outstanding Youth in Conservation 2012, Gloria Barron Prize for Young Heroes 2012, SBN International Youth Award 2013, Greening Forward Earth Savers Club Award 2013, and the YEA! Award for Volunteer/Community Service by Hillsborough County Commissioners 2013.

My connection with nature has always been with me. When I was 9 years old, I was inspired to use that connection to make a difference for all living things and the environment, specifically through frogs and amphibian conservation. Since then, I have had many experiences, traveled in and out of the United States and learned from many people. It's amazing how many people know one another! The large world sometimes seems very small. My project has led to many different doors being opened and all of these opportunities help my environmental voice grow stronger.

What does the word 'magnificent' mean to you?

To me, the word magnificent means great, inspiring and amazing! It can apply to anything, even what some would think of as ordinary. A person who is magnificent would see the possibility of magnificence in everything around him or her. Giant redwood trees are magnificent. Trash can also be magnificent, as it can be reused in many ways. The oak tree in my backyard was magnificent when fully alive, and also after it died, because it gained new life as a snag, providing a new kind of habitat for wildlife. Magnificence is when a humble bee lands on a flower to pollinate it, only then will a fruit or vegetable come from that flower and become our food.

What do you give to the world?

I think all living things are connected from the start, and I think it is very unfair and sad that humans seem to lose their connection with nature, something other species do not seem to do. When people do not believe they are part of the environment, and when they do not think what happens in the natural world affects them, injustice occurs for all living things. The natural world deteriorates and so do people. I help reconnect people and the environment, usually through frogs.

I think of frogs and other non-humans as people, too. I feel sad that their homes are destroyed by someone of my species. The human nature disconnection is the cause of many species disappearing and being imperiled. Because of this, I promised I would do something to help.

I think everyone should feel they are truly interconnected with other living things and the environment. When people feel that connection, they want to help the world and the life in it, not destroy it. A stronger connection means a better life for all living things on Earth.

Why is this important to you?

My beliefs are important to me, and I love sharing them to help make the world a better place. I can't stand to just sit around and do nothing to help the world.

Why did you choose the project/idea that you did?

Basically, the timing of everything was just right. It wasn't something I was looking to do; it just came to me through the different experiences I was having, and I followed it.

Magnificent Kids!

How old were you when you began your project?

9 years old

How did you go about getting it started?

After I started taking the herpetology class and going to frog listening workshops, I also started going to a nature preserve called Camp Bayou Outdoor Learning Center, which is run by a lady named Ms. Dolly Cummings. Everyone who works there is a volunteer, and they really love what they do. They had some home-school classes when I was 9, and we were offered the opportunity to make a display board about our favorite citizen science project for an event they were having. I chose frogs and frog listening and had my first booth for amphibian conservation.

Who is your project benefiting, and how?

My project connects people and the environment, a lot of times through frogs. I share information almost daily on social media and the internet and many times, that information is educational and about a variety of environmental subjects.

When I do a booth or presentation, it may be at a classroom, church, all adult professional conference, nature preserve or community event. My goal is for people to leave feeling empowered and inspired to act and also to feel more connected to all living things on Earth.

'Care Cans' is a ***Conserve It Forward*** project I started in 2013. Each Care Can is filled with messages about nature and artwork from people around the world. The Care Cans go to people who are not able to get outside in nature for a long period of time for some reason. Anyone may recommend somebody to receive a Care Can and they go to individuals who are in and out of hospitals, nursing homes and care centers.

Avalon Theisen

Who were the key people that supported you, and how?

So many people have supported me, including my parents, family, friends, teachers, non-profit organizations, businesses and individuals in the community, both locally and globally. There are so many that I do not want to list names, because I am scared I might leave someone out.

How much financial assistance did you have, and from whom?

When I first started, aged 9, I made and sold bottle cap jewelry and magnets to raise money for my project. At that time, I was also raising money to help buy biosand water filters for people in Kenya through a non-profit organization called Friendly Water for the World.

When I turned 10, I won two awards that included money and this really gave my project a boost. One was the 'Nate the Newt for Amphibian Conservation Award' from SAVE THE FROGS!, and the other was the 'International Young Eco-Hero Award' by Action for Nature.

In 2012, **Conserve It Forward** became a federally recognized non-profit organization. Since then, several people and organizations have made individual donations, which is awesome because every penny goes to program costs. Some awards and grants include:

- Radio Disney Heroes for Change Award
- Disney Friends for Change Grant, Youth Service America
- Save the Frogs! Organizer Package Grant, Gold by SAVE THE FROGS!
- Earth Savers Challenge Grant by Greening Forward

How will you keep your project going into the future?

I will continue to do as I have been doing; growing new projects from ideas when the timing seems right. Financially, I will continue to apply for grants and awards. I believe that if I keep doing what I do, I will be able to keep my project going indefinitely. Maybe I can even keep working for myself when I get out of college.

How have your peers responded to you setting up the project, and do they (or can they) get involved in any way?

All of my friends have been very supportive of my work. Some of them have done things like help at booths, presentations and events. They have done things like run frog themed games, help make treefrog houses for teachers and even created artwork for fundraisers and *Conserve It Forward* Care Cans. Many other kids have helped in these ways too and many of them live far away from me. My website shows many ways for people to become involved, like holding a Human Frog Chorus, making artwork or emailing in their signature for Care Cans cards. They can also make frog habitats, and help share information with their friends and families, among other things. I am always looking for ways to help others get involved and most of them are free or things that almost anyone can do, regardless of age. One of the things I often say is, "If we all do small acts, then together we will make big changes!"

Do you see yourself as ordinary or extraordinary?

Extraordinary! What makes me extraordinary? I am unique, different and willing to stand out from the crowd. Ordinary can be defined as, "with no special or distinctive features," and that is not me. I also think most people are extraordinary in their own way so maybe that means everybody is ordinary, after all. Let's make extraordinary the new ordinary!

What is the most important thing to you?

The two most important things to me are my family and saving the world. I want my generation to be part of what helps make the planet better for future generations.

What are your strengths?

I am loyal, honest, caring and respectful. I always try to figure out how to get things done efficiently, and I'm good at following through with what I say I will do. One of my special strengths is connecting with nature. I love to take time to just watch, listen and feel the natural world around me.

What are your weaknesses?

One of my weaknesses is choosing the right way to say things when people do not understand what I mean. I work through it and usually manage to get my point across, but it is a challenge.

Does your project require you to focus on your strengths?

Yes. It is very important to be honest with my message and actions, because if I am not, people will not believe me. They would not be able to trust in what I am trying to say or do. I am respectful to people who have different beliefs from mine. If they think differently, I try to make sure they leave with some sort of positive experience or knowledge. When I say I am going to do a booth, presentation or event, I make sure I do what I say I am going to do. Even if people do not agree with everything I believe, I hope that they see me as a good ambassador for environmentalism.

Who is your greatest role model and why?

My greatest role model is my mother. She is always at every event in my life and always one of the biggest helping hands. She always takes time to do everything she can to help me. She supports every decision in my life like no one else has.

Of all the people in the world, who inspires you the most?

Of everyone in the world, my family inspires and supports me the most.

Magnificent Kids!

How/where/why did you learn to care globally?

I was born caring about what happens to our Earth and all living things on it. I choose to learn about others, whether a culture on the other side of the world, or an animal in my yard. I keep my connection with nature and other living things by nurturing it. We all share the planet Earth and we must work together to love and protect it.

If you could change one thing in the world, what would it be?

If I could change one thing in the world, I would want to see a world where all living things respect each other. Everything alive feels pain or at least does not want to get hurt. For example, even some trees communicate with each other by sending hormone signals, sometimes as a warning of danger. My theory is they would not do this if they did not feel pain.

What do you think are the ingredients for success?

I think the main ingredients for success are having a great idea and passion for what you want to succeed in, having a plan of how you will accomplish it, people to support you and of course, some financial support, whether it's from someone else or yourself.

What is your global vision?

My global vision is for all living things to live sustainably and at one with the Earth. We were born with a connection with nature, not a separation from nature. My dream is for everyone to respect each other and their different beliefs and uniqueness. We are all individuals that are part of one Earth.

What would be your message to the world?

Let's work together to protect our planet Earth and do everything we can to make sure all living things have a home for many generations to come. It's not just the "cute, furry and fluffy" animals that deserve love. My favorites, the herps (amphibians and reptiles), deserve just as much love as everyone else.

If other kids wanted to start up their own magnificent project, what advice would you give them and what steps would you suggest they take?

The most important thing is to find something you love, and then act on it. Do something to make a positive difference in that area. Make sure to share your project with others and encourage them to help or to make their own positive difference. Doing good and being kind is healthy for everyone.

www.ConserveItForward.org

"Mainly play the things on the piano which please you, even if the teacher does not assign those. That is the way to learn the most, that when you are doing something with such enjoyment that you don't notice that time passes."
~ Letter from Einstein to his son

Carter & Olivia Ries

Carter:

Hi, my name is Carter and I was born in Fayetteville, Georgia. I like soccer (I play goalie), volleyball and swimming. I play the piano and recently started guitar lessons. I have my black belt in Tae Kwon Do and I want to learn archery. I like to read and play games on my iPad. I enjoy travelling and meeting new people from around the world. Someday, I want to be an inventor and help my sister run the world's largest animal sanctuary.

We started *One More Generation (OMG)* back in 2009 when I was 8 ½ and Olivia was 7, in an effort to raise awareness about the plight of endangered species. We teach kids around the world that it is our duty to care for all of God's creations and we show them how they too can make a difference.

In early 2014, I started our latest division called 'We Got You Covered' which is designed to be a vehicle for youth around the world who want to help out in their local communities. Our first initiative was to collect blankets for the homeless. We reached out to Delta airlines and found a way to get several hundred blankets. We are now in the process of having a 'blanket decorating party' where youth from the community get together and help write inspirational quotes of hope on the blankets so the recipients not only get a warm blanket, but also get a message of hope from the youth to let them know they are loved and there is hope for all of us.

'We Got You Covered' will give youth around the world the opportunity to find problems in their own communities that they would like to get involved in. We will help them with resources and suggestions on how they can help. We hope to provide the youth with an outlet to make a difference and show them that getting involved in helping others is easier than they may have thought.

Olivia:

Hi, my name is Olivia and I too was born in Fayetteville, Georgia. I like being on the swim team and playing volleyball. I also like to read (a lot) and play piano. I like travelling around the world and helping animals everywhere I go. I want to be a large animal vet someday and help my brother run the world's largest animal sanctuary. We started **OMG** to help save animals and along the way learned that we also need to help clean up our environment so all the animals (and people) have a safe and clean place to live.

In 2013, I also started the *'GreenWell'* division of **OMG**. I grow organic produce that I donate to local animal rescue centers that need healthy produce for their animal guests. We have already donated food from the *'GreenWell'* Garden to our local aquarium and other animal organizations. Excess produce is then delivered to our local senior home. I hope to someday make *'GreenWell'* available to kids all around the country who could search a database of organizations in their home towns that they could supply produce to.

Carter & Olivia:

OMG's other programs help communities tackle environmental issues such as Plastic Pollution and animal conservation issues like the poaching of rhinos, which is pushing the species to the brink of extinction. We engage and empower students and their families by offering solutions that can make a difference. We also have our 'Plastic Awareness Coalition' that now has over 70 local, national and even international partners who are all helping us to find ways to reduce the amount of plastic pollution we generate.

Among many awards and honors, we have won the grand prize for Nestles Heroes Award, received recognition for our video as an inspiration for the organization started by Miley Cyrus called 'Get Ur Good On', and we were chosen as one of the 10 Most Inspiring Student Activists by OnlineDegrees.org. We also received the International Youth in Philanthropy Award and the 2013 Partner of the Year, awarded by the Fulton County School District for our programs that engage youth around the world. While we don't like to boast about our honors, we do appreciate that our work is being noticed and hope this will inspire other young people to make a difference.

OMG has appeared in magazines and newspapers both nationally and internationally, including The Wall Street Journal, The New York Times and the Los Angeles Times. We have also appeared on TV including CNN and USA Today, but our most exciting moment was when Steve Harvey invited us to join him on his show. We talked a lot about the trip we were just about to take to South Africa to make a documentary about the rhinos. We have since traveled to South Africa with a film crew from Red Sky Productions and we are currently working on the launch of the documentary. While it was amazing to see the rhinos close up and experience a connection with them, it was also very sad to see mother rhinos that had been killed by poachers in front of their babies. We are working really hard to raise awareness about this so that one day the poaching will stop. But we have to hurry because the Western Black rhino already became extinct in 2013, and the Northern White rhino and the Javan rhino are also very close to extinction.

Since returning from our trip, the baby black rhino that we visited at the rhino orphanage (and is featured in the documentary trailer) had to be put down. The young rhino sustained a leg injury while trying to protect her mother from the poachers and the injury was too severe, causing the baby rhino unbearable and constant pain. Rhino-poaching is still a big problem and the poachers have also killed several of the rhinos we visited while filming in South Africa.

Upon returning from South Africa, we learned that the Dallas Safari Hunting Club was planning on auctioning off a permit to shoot and kill a critically endangered black rhino. The Dallas Safari Club claims this auction was to help Animal Conservation. The Namibian government sold five permits to allow hunters to come and shoot rhinos that they deemed were no longer productive to the crash (a crash is a group of rhinos, like a herd is a group of elephants). Often, governments will allow these permits to kill such animals. People with lots of money and no compassion, compete for the right to kill such a rare species.

Once we heard about the auction, we travelled to Dallas to try to meet with the President of the Dallas Safari Hunting Club to see if we could convince him to cancel the auction. He ignored all of our calls and emails and when we confronted him at the convention center, he turned and ran like a chicken and had security escort us away from the entrance. Later, while we were trying to discuss our position with the folks attending the event, the police escorted us out of the building.

We also participated in a local protest by others who agreed with our position. It was so frustrating because there were many people who drove by and honked at us and yelled things like 'Go Kill The Rhinos!' It made Olivia cry at first but then she just became more determined to tell the world how ridiculous the auction was.

Once we returned from Dallas, we found out who the winner of the auction was and that he paid $350,000.00 to buy the permit. Olivia sat down and wrote the winner a letter asking him if he would agree to Skype with us so we could try to talk some sense into him. We posted the letter on our FaceBook page and within hours, we had over a thousand messages of support from people all over the world who agreed with us.

Our reason for going to Dallas was not about us being 'anti-hunting'. We went to Dallas to teach others that the old methods of animal conservation, which are used to control populations of abundant species, should not be used when dealing with a critically endangered species like the black rhino. Every time someone tries to tell us that we are too young to understand or that we have no clue about what the issue is, we ask them this simple question, 'How low do the numbers have to get before you will agree that we can no longer afford to lose even one more rhino?' There are less than 5,000 black rhinos left in the wild. 'Do they have to get down to 2,000 before we say enough is enough? What about when we are down to only 500? Will that finally get you to agree we need to find alternatives other than shooting them?' So far, no one has answered our questions.

We will be featuring the actual Skype call we had with the winner of the auction in our documentary, along with our plans to travel to Vietnam and China to continue teaching youth of the world why we need to save rhinos for future generations.

Together, we travel anywhere from 30,000 - 50,000 miles each year in our *OMG* van, around the region/country and host community outreach education programs that teach everyone about the need to get involved. Our main goal is to show others that anybody can make a difference... if we can, you can too!

What does the word 'magnificent' mean to you?

Carter: Magnificent to me means 'amazing, broad or open'. It means that you can make a difference.

Olivia: Magnificent to me means 'amazing', like all of God's creatures and like the people who care about them.

What do you give to the world?

Carter: I kind of think that I give hope and inspiration to the world and that we do this through education.

Olivia: I think I give help, love and kindness to others, and that is what I give to the world.

Why is this important to you?

Carter: Because the animals and our planet need more people to care.

Olivia: Because there are so many people who only care for themselves and not for others or for animals. I want to show them that giving help, love and kindness is a good thing, and that we should all try it.

Why did you choose the project/idea that you did?

Carter: We decided to start *OMG* to help save animals and to clean up our environment.

Olivia: Because I love animals and I want to protect them for generations to come.

How old were you when you began your project?

Carter: 8.5 years old.

Olivia: 7 years old.

How did you go about getting it started?

Carter: We started by seeking out projects to get involved with and by asking for help. We tell kids everywhere that if they too want to make a difference, they need to tell every adult they know about their passion and not to give up until the adults give in.

Olivia: We started by researching about which animals needed help and trying to find a way we could get involved. We then just didn't stop until we got adults to help us get started.

Who is your project benefiting, and how?

Carter: Mainly kids and animals. By teaching our peers about the need to get involved, we are ensuring that the animals have someone who will help protect them however they can.

Olivia: The animals and communities are the ones who benefit from our work. We teach people how to care for the animals and their environment, and we all win.

Who were the key people that supported you, and how?

Carter: We have been fortunate to attract the support of several major sponsors who learned about us and decided to help us with grants or other forms of support.

Olivia: Our parents and other family members were the ones who helped us get started. Now we partner with other organizations to find ways we can help each other accomplish our goals.

How much financial assistance did you have, and from whom?

Carter: There never seems to be enough financial support to do all the things we want, but so far we have managed because of donations and from sponsorship from several key companies like Novelis, the Turner Foundation, the Dee Little Foundation and from the Captain Planet Foundation.

Olivia: Funding has been hard to come by but so far we have managed. We really rely on donations and welcome every cent we can get. Our parents paid for all of the initial start-up costs and they still have to chip in but someday we hope our organization can take care of itself.

How will you keep your project going into the future?

Carter: We will continue to ask for donations and try to organize fundraisers etc. We will also continue to seek corporate sponsorship wherever possible. We will be launching a Youth Membership Program soon that will allow youth of the world to get involved and help make a difference.

Olivia: With passion. We started *OMG* because we are so passionate and I believe that will help us get what we need to continue.

How have your peers responded to you setting up the project, and do they (or can they) get involved in any way?

Carter: Most of them are very supportive and we always try to show them how they too can make a difference by adopting animals or writing letters to officials or just by speaking up at their school about what they have learned and what they care about.

Olivia: Some of my peers are very passionate about what we do and some seem almost jealous because of all the cool places we have been and the amazing people we have met.

Do you see yourself as ordinary or extraordinary?

Carter: Ordinary. We get asked that a lot and our parents get people constantly telling them how we are so special etc. I just think what we are doing is what everyone should be doing! We have made it our job to prove that to other kids.

Olivia: Ordinary!!! I don't like it when people say we are special or different. Most of the kids we know are the same as us. They all have a passion for something and some are ready to follow their passions and some are not, it doesn't make them any less special than anyone else.

What is the most important thing to you?

Carter: To save as many animals as we can and to teach people to clean up our environment for everyone.

Olivia: Family, Animals, School and Friends... in that order ;-)

What are your strengths?

Carter: I am not sure yet. My parents tell me that I am very compassionate and that is why we work so hard at trying to make a difference but I don't know if that is a strength or just something I was born with.

Olivia: I think one of my strengths is that I love to read and research about animals and that I was born with a caring heart. It makes me feel good to know I am helping animals.

What are your weaknesses?

Carter: I am not sure what to answer for this question. I think I get nervous when making presentations sometimes and that is a weakness but my parents tell me it is normal and only shows that I care enough to want to do well.

Olivia: I get so frustrated when I see or hear about people hurting animals, or any living thing for that matter. I recently wrote a letter to my teacher asking her to please never again kill insects that she finds around the school because they deserve to live just like us. She agreed to try.

Does your project require you to focus on your strengths?

Carter: Yes, I think that if you want to be successful, you need to use all of your strengths, even if you are not sure what they are. Just do the best you can and you will make a difference.

Olivia: I agree with Carter, the more research we do about the project we are about to do, the more confident we are and the more we can get people to listen and hopefully start caring as well.

Who is your greatest role model and why?

Carter: I really admire Dr. Silvia Earl (she is considered one of the world's foremost experts within the Marine environment) and I would one-day love to work with her on ways we can clean up our oceans. I also admire Dr. Jane Goodall and Dr. Birute Galdikas who we will be working with on our next big project. I am so excited.

Olivia: God, because he made people to look after all of the animals.

Of all the people in the world, who inspires you the most?

Carter: We recently met an amazing lady who has an even bigger heart for animals than we do. She told us about her animals at home and how her baby cow had a broken leg but she refused to put it down. She said she cares so much for the animal that she could never get rid of it. She also fights to get companies to stop animal testing. My parents won't let us see what companies are doing to these poor animals but they said that what this incredible lady is doing is amazing and we should be thankful that God made people like her.

Olivia: My parents. They believe in us and they allow us to do what we want to do to make a difference.

How/where/why did you learn to care globally?

Carter: During the Gulf oil spill, my sister and I spent four months collecting badly needed animal rescue supplies and then we drove down to the region and spent five days helping out with the rescue efforts. While we were there, a professor from Berkeley CA thanked us for our work but then asked what we were doing about the environment. We did not understand why she was asking and we actually were surprised that she was asking because it was as if she was saying we were not doing enough. That is when she explained that without some sort of environmental program, we were basically spinning our wheels. She then told us about the issue of Plastic Pollution and most of the animals we helped nurture back to good health were going to encounter some sort of plastic pollution and that many would either become entangled in it or die from ingesting it. That is when we realized that there were issues out there that were truly global and we decided to get involved for the sake of all the animals all over the world.

Olivia: I think the desire to want to help all animals all over the world comes from my heart. I don't know how else to explain it. I just want to help them all.

If you could change one thing in the world, what would it be?

Carter: I would try to find a way to stop greed. Every time we learn about another problem or about another manufacturer who is making a product in a packaging that is not recyclable or environmentally friendly, it always seems to boil down to a company choosing profits over what is right for our environment or for the animals. If I could change one thing, I think that would be it.

Olivia: I would like to find a way to change people so that they all would care for others and for all of the animals. I just cannot understand how you can go through life not caring about anything except yourself.

What do you think are the ingredients for success?

Carter: Never give up, be positive (even if you are working on a project that is depressing to think about) and always be kind to others, even if they don't get it.

Olivia: You have to have passion, never give up and always believe in yourself.

What is your global vision?

Carter: Someday we want to truly have the world's largest animal sanctuary. We would use these facilities to not only provide a safe haven for all of the animals; we would also use this as an educational vehicle to teach everyone about the need to save these animals and that we all need to care.

Olivia: I envision our animal sanctuary as a place where we can teach people to care and to be passionate about all of God's creations.

What would be your message to the world?

Carter: 'Anybody can make a difference… if we can, you can too.'

Olivia: 'Anybody can make a difference… if we can, you can too'. Seriously, that is what we want everyone to understand.

If other kids wanted to start up their own magnificent project, what advice would you give them and what steps would you suggest they take?

Carter: Just Do It!!! Take the first step. Find your passion and do some research on it. Get to know as much as you can about the subject and then look for ways to get started. We also encourage youth around the world to join our Youth Membership Program. We have already added divisions to **OMG** such as *'GreenWell'* and *'We've Got You Covered'*, which provide an opportunity for those with other passions and interests to get involved. It doesn't matter if you are passionate about animals, the environment or about helping in your community, **One More Generation** is a Youth Empowerment company and we aim to help the next generation of leaders to find their passion and their voice.

Olivia: Follow your heart and get your parents to do the same. Tell every adult in your family what you're passionate about and keep telling them. Eventually they will see that you are serious and they will help you get started.

If you are unsure about what you might want to get involved with, or you need some ideas about how you can make a difference, join **One More Generation** as a Team Member for stories, fun facts and tips about the projects we are working on and how you can get involved in your community.

http://onemoregeneration.org

"Do not go where the path may lead, go instead where there is no path and leave a trail"
~ Ralph Waldo Emerson

Clover Hogan

My name is Clover, and I go to the greenest school on earth. I was born in Australia, but moved to the island of Bali in Indonesia two years ago. The environment I'm living in now encourages me to pursue my passion for writing and journalism specifically. I'm in the midst of writing a fiction novel, I have created two animal activist documentaries in the last year and I am collaborating with people from all over the world to make a difference on this planet.

The first documentary was focused on the welfare of Bali dogs, which through social media received an international response. The second documentary was about vegetarianism and has just been released. I believe that two of my greatest purposes in life are to provide a voice for the voiceless and to spread knowledge and awareness throughout our beautiful world.

I wanted to find the reason behind the terrible state of dog welfare and being an activist, I wanted to do everything I could to help these animals. I worked with an extraordinary organisation called the Bali Animal Welfare Association (BAWA), which rescues thousands of animals on the island each year. After 6 months of researching the issue, I posted my documentary on YouTube. It quickly resonated with many people around the world, with requests to have it screened at an animal fundraiser hosted by Kerri-Anne Kennerly in Australia, and airing on Canadian TV as part of a special program on the Green School. I'm really happy to have achieved my original intention, which was to 'provide a voice for the voiceless.'

The Bali dog has been around for over 5,000 years and is the true ancestor of the very first proto dog that evolved from wolves. Out of all the dog breeds in the world, the Bali dog holds the richest pool of genetic diversity. In Hindu society, Bali dogs have been highly valued as guard dogs and sometimes used in sacrifices. In 2008 Bali experienced an outbreak of rabies and tens of thousands of dogs were poisoned or killed. With the help of BAWA and other animal welfare groups, education programs are being conducted in the hope that rabies can be managed from a firm foundation of knowledge rather than fear. Until recently, the Bali dog has managed to live parallel to humans with mutual respect for each other. While rabies is now almost under control in Bali, the inhumane treatment of these animals is an ongoing issue.

It is my hope that by creating the Bali Dog documentary, humans will be more considerate, respectful and aware of the lives they share this planet with, and make a more conscious effort to treat other living creatures with compassion and respect. Hopefully, it will also inspire people to volunteer or get involved in working towards a solution.

Service is about helping others, but in doing so, you are also projecting happiness into your own life, which is one of the many benefits. One of the service projects that I am currently working on concerns stray dogs on the island of Bali. It involves working at a shelter and raising awareness through my own endeavours, such as the Bali Dogs documentary.

What does the word 'magnificent' mean to you?

To me, the definition of magnificent is something that's brilliant and fantastically grand.

What do you give to the world?

I think I give passion to the world and share a genuine love for our environment with the people around me. I do everything to the best of my ability and always strive to put my heart and soul into the things I love.

Why is this important to you?

I believe passion is an essential element in life and happiness. It's one thing to be alive; another to *feel* alive.

Why did you choose the project/idea that you did?

Anyone on the island can clearly see that the Bali dogs are in a lot of trouble and in need of serious help. It seemed to be the biggest and most relevant issue and I knew that I could contribute to the Bali community through this specific project.

How old were you when you began your project?

I was 13. I started the project in January 2013, just months before my 14th birthday in June.

How did you go about getting it started?

It was rather tricky to get the project up and running in the beginning, as I had no set structure in place and I wasn't even sure of what I wanted to achieve by the end of the 6 month block. But with the support of my family and external groups such as BAWA, I set out my ambitions and before long, I was on my way to achieving those goals.

Who is your project benefiting, and how?

My project has benefited the Bali dogs and spread awareness, not only to the people within Bali who are being affected, but also people in other countries.

Who were the key people that supported you, and how?

As my mentor for the Quest program run by my school, my sister Hayley was there to support me the most. My whole family contributed with their knowledge and experience with writing and media, especially my mum throughout the writing and researching process. I wouldn't have been able to complete my hours and work at BAWA if it weren't for Hayley's partner, Ivor, who volunteered at the clinic with me. He was fine with his position as a cage cleaner, while I played with the gorgeous little puppies. Lastly, BAWA itself helped me greatly and the project wouldn't have received nearly as much attention without the association and the many great people working within it.

How much financial assistance did you have, and from whom?

I didn't have or need any financial assistance apart from fuel to drive to the clinic, which my parents covered.

How will you keep your project going into the future?

Well, very unfortunately, the BAWA clinic and ambulance service has actually been shut down by the government, for private reasons. This was incredibly upsetting, especially after witnessing all of the good that the organisation had done, and they were such a major link in the chain of my project, but I suppose I'll still try to do whatever I can on the awareness front, by sharing my video.

How have your peers responded to you setting up the project, and do they (or can they) get involved in any way?

All of my friends have been supportive of the project by sharing the video on their social media pages, but I think that they were all pretty involved in their own Quest projects when the documentary was released.

Do you see yourself as ordinary or extraordinary?

I don't see myself as either ordinary or extraordinary; I see it instead as a case of a normal (not so ordinary?) girl, in a great environment, striving to achieve extraordinary things.

What is the most important thing to you?

The most important thing to me would have to be family. I definitely wouldn't have achieved half of the things I have so far without the love and support they've provided.

What are your strengths?

The things I admire in myself are the compassion that I have for all creatures and my determination that allows me to work through troubling issues.

What are your weaknesses?

Procrastination would have to be one of my biggest weaknesses, although I must admit that I work best under pressure.

Does your project require you to focus on your strengths?

Absolutely. I witnessed some rather troubling things throughout the project, but it was my compassion that led me there in the first place, and determination that allowed me to work through it.

Who is your greatest role model and why?

That's a tough question... I'd have to say my greatest role model (regarding environmentalism especially) would have to be my sister, Hayley. I became a vegetarian and developed a real awareness of nature because of her, but my whole family has definitely contributed to that.

Of all the people in the world, who inspires you the most?

I think that my mum, Janet, probably inspires me the most. We're so different from each other but we get along like two peas in a pod and I've only recently come to terms with how truly remarkable she is. She has this lovely aura and happy energy that seems to just rub off on everyone and I really admire her ability to find light and good in everything. My family is always sending her up for being "Guru Jandhi," because of how spiritual she is, but she just laughs at herself no matter what.

How/where/why did you learn to care globally?

Green School has really encouraged me to think globally and develop a totally different outlook on the world. Where I came from in regional Australia, the focus was very local and before moving overseas, I definitely didn't have this consciousness that we are all living on this planet together and that we can create change if we believe in it strongly enough.

If you could change one thing in the world, what would it be?

I would change the world so that all living creatures were treated with equality.

What do you think are the ingredients for success?

You have to believe in yourself and have confidence in the goal you're striving toward.

What is your global vision?

One day, I wish to live in an entirely aware world with the human race respecting the planet and all creatures equally.

What would be your message to the world?

Respect all life, because it is precious, and share love with the world.

If other kids wanted to start up their own magnificent project, what advice would you give them and what steps would you suggest they take?

Once again, I'd say believe in yourself and what you're trying to accomplish. Have confidence in your project and make sure that your number one intention is to bring about good. Firstly, you need to set out your intentions and make sure that they are realistic in the

Magnificent Kids!

given circumstances. That's not to say don't think big; the more people and things that you're positively affecting, the better. Once you have your goals down, plan as many things out as possible and have all of your structures in place. I can guarantee that your plans will change along the way, but you're sure to save a lot of hard work and time if they're there. Make sure you have support behind you; it's healthy to need help, especially when everything becomes overwhelming. Finally, have fun! That's what everyone says, but in the end, it's true. Be passionate and stay positive with your project.

http://clover-hogan.weebly.com/

Dallas Jessup

"Dallas Jessup may be only 22 years old, but she knows how to change the world. She is an accomplished filmmaker, author, speaker and trainer, and grew a local community service project into the international nonprofit *Just Yell Fire* – now a million-girl revolution across 66 countries".

Hi, I'm Dallas Jessup. As a 13-year-old black belt martial artist, I learned the frightening statistics that 1 in 4 girls will be sexually assaulted and that there are 114,000 attempted abductions each year in the U.S. alone. I set out to create a home movie to teach my schoolmates at Portland, Oregon's St. Mary's Academy High School, some street-fighting techniques to defend themselves. Word spread that a young girl was putting together an important film and in 60 days I had a 30-member volunteer professional crew, 100 volunteer extras, celebrity cameos by Josh Holloway and Evangeline Lilly and $600,000 in donated resources. These efforts culminated in the 46-minute film *"Just Yell Fire"*. It teaches girls how to literally fight back against predators and sexual assault.

Magnificent Kids!

I posted the film online as a free download and raised funds to produce and ship DVDs to girls without internet access. The film received nearly one million downloads in two years and multiple awards, including American Library Association's Most Notable Video designation. I have traveled an average of 10,000 miles a month and my nonprofit organization provides teen safety programs, training and presentations for high schools, colleges, camps, women's events and crisis shelters throughout the U.S. and many countries around the world. The original film is still available for free download or DVD for any girl, worldwide.

As a student at Vanderbilt University, I saw a need for a film that addresses the unique dangers girls and young women face in college. My second film, *"Just Yell Fire: Campus Life"*, was filmed at the end of my sophomore year and launched the following spring. *"Just Yell Fire: Campus Life"* teaches girls their rights and how to identify, avoid or escape dating violence, hall cruising, parking lot dangers, date rape, date rape drugs and jogging dangers. I teamed up with my fraternity AOII on a national level and worked with colleges across the country. Massachusetts Institute of Technology teaches *'Just Yell Fire'* as a credited course and the program has been integrated on over 200 campuses.

I have been called to testify before congress, and traveled as far away as India to teach my techniques to girls in 12 colleges throughout Southern India. The program has been endorsed by governors, senators, congress, attorney generals and more across the U.S. and Canada.

Awards: CNN Hero, Hall of Fame for Caring Americans, Presidents Youth Service Award, Points of Light Award, Elle Girl Teen Hero, Do Something Award, Prudential Washington State Volunteer of the Year, Caring Award, World of Children Award, Huggable Hero, Jefferson Award, Kohl's Kids Who Care National Award and many others.

Media Appearances: Good Morning America, Today Show, ABC News, MSNBC, Fox News Live, Fox and Friends, People Magazine, The New York Times, USA Today, Teen Magazine,

Seventeen Magazine, Glamour Magazine, NPR, Bust Magazine and many other TV, Radio, Magazine and Newspapers around the world.

I can't imagine my life without **Just Yell Fire**. I have had amazing experiences, had dinner with Governors of several states in the US and shepherds in India. I have worked with at risk girls 'in the system' and privileged private school girls. I have met celebrities, movie and television stars, super models, as well as the poorest street kids in Mexico and every one of them has taught me something valuable. If you are open to learning from everyone you meet, the scope of your life will expand beyond your wildest dreams. Don't be afraid to go for it. One of the most important things I have learned is the true definition of a hero. It is the person who does the right thing, even if they are afraid to do it… especially if they are afraid to do it.

What does the word 'magnificent' mean to you?

Am I on an episode of "Are You Smarter Than a 5th Grader"? But seriously, magnificent describes something that despite the obstacles, despite the naysayers it is something or someone that rose above the negativity and doubt to shine and truly make an impact in an outstanding, jaw dropping way.

What do you give to the world?

Just Yell Fire provides the educational tools to help girls avoid becoming the 1 in 3 who will be in a violent dating relationship, the 1 in 4 who will statistically be raped before graduating from college and the many other statistics which illustrate how women are vulnerable and at a disadvantage. Most girls do not have the time, money, or want to put in the effort to dedicate to years and years of martial arts. *Just Yell Fire* provides that beginning platform, breaking down martial arts to its core to illustrate how to get out of a bad situation as quickly as possible.

Why is this important to you?

Just Yell Fire is so important because there's so much out there for the aftermath, which of course is needed, but very little focus on the prevention of violence. It's unfortunate but in the rape, abduction and assault category, many people would rather deal with the victims rather than prevention. We've heard from several girls who have got themselves out of bad situations because of seeing one of our two films and that's what keeps the momentum going – knowing we're able to help girls and young women get out of violent situations.

Why did you choose the project/idea that you did?

Watching the news with my family when I was a freshman in high school, I saw the surveillance video of a young girl in Florida. She was about my age so it resonated and in the video, a man came up to her and grabbed her arm. She looked at him, it appeared as if he spoke to her and she walked away with him. Four days later her body was found. With a black belt in Tae Kwon Do and a 2nd Degree Instructorship in Filipino Street Fighting, I knew that Carlie Brucia didn't have to die. The injustice made me angry and I combined it with the skill set I had to help create real change. What makes truly successful social causes is this combination because it gives you the drive to use your talents to get things done.

Dallas Jessup

How old were you when you began your project?

I was 13 when I saw the video of Carlie Brucia and the process began. We filmed the original *"Just Yell Fire"* film when I was 14 and the film was launched that October.

How did you go about getting it started?

After seeing the video of Carlie Brucia who was taken and found dead four days later, I did some research and found out that 1 in 4 girls will be raped before they graduate from college. I thought I could make a homemade video showing a few techniques so that my friends would not have to experience this. I attended an all girl's high school. Through my research I began to realize that of the 650 girls at my high school, statistically 162 of them could be raped and that angered me. Especially since there were several high profile abductions and murders near my hometown and some friends were asking my advice as to what they could do to get out of an attack situation. Once I told my mother about my idea she encouraged me to take a script writing class at a local community college. The professor loved the project and said he might have some friends in the industry who would love to help a cause like this. After talking to several people, we got a professional crew of 30, 40 film students to act as assistants to the director, sound engineer, gaffer, lights, and more. Students ran cameras B, C and D, we had 100 extras (friends) and we reached out to ABC's cast of LOST and were able to get Evangeline Lilly and Josh Holloway to do cameos for the film. We planned out the film and found all the resources, filmed for a week, edited and put the film online as a free download in October of 2006. *"Just Yell Fire"* received national and global attention as the media picked up the story and helped us spread our message.

Who is your project benefiting, and how?

Our project benefits everyone in a different capacity. We help empower young women to learn their rights and how to stand up for themselves if they are attacked. We help bring some peace of mind to parents, brothers and cousins who are concerned for their female friends and relatives. We help mothers who are concerned for their daughters, especially if they had been a victim of sexual assault themselves. Despite how great teachers, parents and policemen are, they cannot be everywhere and *Just Yell Fire* helps young women learn how to take control of their own outcome in those situations.

Who were the key people that supported you, and how?

Many people helped. My parents did so much, but neighbours pitched in with equipment, money, etc. Friends helped on the set and came in as extras. Clackamas Community College let us use their campus for most of our location shots and their film students got class credit for working on the film. Takafumi Uehara, our director, not only directed both films but he edited them, for free. Local film supply companies loaned us some really expensive cameras, MVT Productions in Santa Ana, California shot the 2nd film for cost. University of California at Irvine loaned us their campus and dorms for the 2nd film, *"Just Yell Fire: Campus Life"*. Celebrities volunteered: everyone from Evangeline Lilly and Josh Holloway in *"Just Yell Fire"* to Shay Mitchell, Jonathan Jackson, Karina Smirnoff, Jake Gleeson (he's from New Zealand and plays on the Portland Timbers Soccer Team), Tinsel Korey and so many more let us use their celebrity with the hope that more girls would pay attention.

There are many, many more people who helped and supported us and this kind of project simply cannot be done without the help and kindness of many people. St. Mary's Academy in Portland, Oregon where I went to high school also played a significant role in our success. They allowed me to send my homework in via email, to take tests either early or late as needed for the travel I was doing and they made sure I never fell behind. Vanderbilt University was also supportive in every way. I received an enormous scholarship and the professors and staff worked with me to make sure I could meet my obligations and keep up with my studies. They helped me throughout the process when I was called to testify before Congress, even sending a representative to walk me through it all and using the

Vanderbilt Public Policy Office in Washington DC to make sure protocol was followed. This was very much appreciated as I was an 18-year-old freshman and didn't have a clue how that whole process worked.

How much financial assistance did you have, and from whom?

Our original film was estimated at $600,000+ to film, produce, edit etc. but with talent, locations, equipment and labour donated, we were able to produce *"Just Yell Fire"* with a little over $6,000. The organization has run on donations, grants, awards and fees for presentations and training. We do have an online store where we sell DVDs, books and drug test coasters. The money raised goes to producing more products and keeping the doors open. Everyone on staff is a volunteer, so we don't have large overhead costs. *"Just Yell Fire: Campus Life"* cost us approximately $15,000 to produce, but the estimate of what it would cost if we had to pay for everything is well over one million dollars. This money was donated by friends and family.

How will you keep your project going into the future?

We have a train-the-trainer program, which certifies leaders in the community, teachers, police officers and campus security to teach our program. We keep looking for new people to help us grow our program. With *"Just Yell Fire: Campus Life"* we've created several partnerships like our one with Alpha Omicron Pi International Women's Fraternity and Tix4Cause, which is an organization that donates 42% of their service charge from ticket sales for concerts, sporting events, theatre and much more. This is a very good way for anyone to do good by buying tickets they would buy anyway, they just buy them through our site and we get a sizeable donation. The best part about this is the tickets cost no more than they would on any other ticket selling site.

How have your peers responded to you setting up the project, and do they (or can they) get involved in any way?

Our first film wouldn't have been complete without my friends stepping up and helping as extras, production help and much more. Since then, many people have helped spread the word, with fundraisers, setting up events in their hometowns, helping with presentations, and more. I have continual support from my friends within *Just Yell Fire*, who send me notes from classes I miss while travelling for *Just Yell Fire*. I owe them a lot of thanks for all of their volunteer work and personal support.

Do you see yourself as ordinary or extraordinary?

When I first started, it was cool getting local and national press and being in high demand as a speaker and it was easy to think that this was something new and different. As I started winning awards I met 100s of other kids working to improve our world. Some of them are as 'googleable' as Jennifer Lawrence and others are unsung heroes. However, what I have seen is that my generation, for all the smack it's been given about being slackers and the entitlement generation, is gibberish. Society tends to focus on the bad but if you look around, every kid really wants to help make a difference in our world today. We all have causes that speak to us personally and we just want to help. Some of us just get more encouragement than others so we're able to follow through. I wouldn't say I'm ordinary or extraordinary, I'd say I'm pleased to be a part of the Revolution of Compassion that is my generation.

What is the most important thing to you?

Relationships. The world is already so large and is often confusing. Communications with friends, family, boyfriends and professional relationships constantly teach you things. They teach you how to love, they teach you how to care for others, they teach you about choosing different paths – pretty much all lessons in life are based on relationships. Humans are meant to interact with one another and even though being an independent young lady is important, it does not mean you do not care for others. Without my friends, family, past boyfriends and business partners *Just Yell Fire* would not have been successful and I wouldn't have learned as much as I have. So thank you to everyone who has ever taught me something, good or bad and helped me grow as an individual.

What are your strengths?

The answer to this question depends who you ask. As much as possible I try to keep my personal life and professional life separate but at the heart of it, I'm always just Dallas. Being a Communication Studies major at Vanderbilt along with leading a global non-profit, I have gained a diverse range of skills from being able to write press releases, to getting people to care about a social injustice, to rhetorically analysing a president's speech, to always being there for my friends. At the heart of it, I believe I'm great at recognizing others' strengths and finding ways to use those strengths in combination with what I have learned, to help them create effective social change around the globe. I also help my friends achieve their goals – or at least give them my loyal support.

What are your weaknesses?

Weaknesses? I'm impatient when things take longer than expected and I am a truly caring person which is always a battle between gut, mind and heart.

Does your project require you to focus on your strengths?

Any successful project requires you to focus on your strengths. It's also important to recognize when to bring in people if you don't have the necessary skills. Throughout the production of both of our films, we brought together people from various paths and areas of expertise to create one final product. You can't do that alone. Part of being strong is recognizing what you can do and to ask for help and bring in talent where you have gaps.

Magnificent Kids!

Who is your greatest role model and why?

I don't know that I have one particular role model. My life and my path have been influenced by so many. Teachers and Mrs. Dowling in Kindergarten who taught me that I could do anything I wanted in life. Professors mentored me in so many ways and made sure I knew that the world is not so big and that I have a lot of power. My parents backed my play and made sure I knew I was never alone and they would always be there no matter what I decided to do. Friends have stood by me and propped me up whenever I needed it. I guess if I had to name one person whom I would consider a role model, it would be Nicholas Zeppos, Chancellor of Vanderbilt University. This man has tremendous responsibility. He has to deal with thousands of undergrad and graduate students, alumni, parents, board members, faculty and staff, yet he is always available. He has an open door policy, knows everyone's name, (truly every student, parent and staff member), he is a father, has a very prestigious position yet is frequently seen in jeans helping with a project or playing the guitar with the band at a school concert. He never ceases to amaze me and always seems to be in a great mood.

Of all the people in the world, who inspires you the most?

I have been inspired by my parents, a number of amazing Vanderbilt professors and passionate world changers I meet as the founder of a non-profit. For a well-recognized role model: Diane Sawyer as she has mastered an influential and challenging profession while maintaining dignity, style and a happy family life.

How/where/why did you learn to care globally?

As a family we have always travelled. My parents made sure that we saw the museums and tourist attractions, but they also made sure we saw the real life of whatever city, state or country we were visiting. I was never allowed to eat at an American Chain restaurant when we were in another country. We ate what the locals ate. We mingled and integrated with people of all levels and I was always taught to treat people with respect. My parents taught me to treat the housekeeper with the same respect as the Attorney General who has been a guest in our home. I was taught that we are very fortunate as a family and the worst thing I could ever do is to use my good fortune to hurt anyone. I was never allowed to make someone feel bad if they didn't have the same clothes, house, experiences or whatever. Race and social position has never been a part of our lives. I was taught that everyone is doing the best they can with what they have to work with and the only people they consider lower than others are those who judge people and think of themselves as better. As I have grown, I see their point. So, globally, if you believe everyone is doing the best they can with what they have to work with, then you must also believe that by giving them more to work with, they can do more. You never know if our next Nobel Prize winner will be someone you helped and maybe this will happen because you helped.

If you could change one thing in the world, what would it be?

I would change the tendency for adults to dismiss young people's ideas. Adults view youth as idealistic and unrealistic kids who have no idea of the complexities of the world. This is true but it is also true that kids view things with unbiased opinions and haven't been jaded. They simply don't know 'it can't be done'. This is why so many start-ups today are by people in their 20s. We limit our future growth by instilling a mindset of "this is the way it is" and there is nothing you can do to change that. Society needs to break the shackles that are tying us down to the status quo and allow kids to do as Seth Godin says, "Be different to be better."

What do you think are the ingredients for success?

Ingredients for success in life? There is no easy answer to that because success is different for everyone. Some will find success in their jobs, some in their home lives and others by changing the world. At its core, success is about being happy with your circumstances and yourself and waking up feeling excited to live your life. So the secret to success is: do what makes you happy and realize no one can make you feel inferior without your consent. As long as you're doing what drives you (obviously if it's not hurting others) then you are a positive contributing member of society and that is success. For me I found that by not taking myself too seriously and helping others, I became a much better person.

What is your global vision?

I think globally we need to move past our misconceptions, biases and fear of things we do not understand and the only way to do this is to learn more about other cultures and other people for ourselves. We need to move past tolerance of people who are different from us and truly engage in the acceptance of it. You do not need to believe in someone else's religion or government but society needs to take the time to learn the facts and be open to discussion. I've celebrated Hanukah, spent Thanksgiving in Canada and discussed the inner workings of Jainism. None of these experiences have changed my personal views but it helps me understand other cultures and appreciate them for being unique and interesting. Globally, we need to engage with each other and open up pathways. People are not born to be racist, to fear or with biases; these are things that are taught by society and if we hope to ever begin to achieve world peace we have to stop passing these concepts on. We need to accept people for who they are and allow them to accept us.

What would be your message to the world?

Find that thing that resonates with you, makes your reality better than your dreams and stick to it. It may not be within the world of social impact but we need a global shift of a proud, driven community who brings us into the future. Don't be content with the status quo; if you see something wrong, change it. If everyone, everywhere, just changed one thing for the better, everything would get better. I have found that there are three kinds of people in the world: those who make things happen, those who let things happen and those who wonder what just happened. Be the one who makes things happen.

If other kids wanted to start up their own magnificent project, what advice would you give them and what steps would you suggest they take?

1) Ask what social injustice makes you angry. This is the cause you should take on and the cause for which you'll have the guts and motivation to create real change.

2) Acknowledge your strengths and your weaknesses. Find others who excel at your weaknesses and ask them for help. People truly want to help a kid who is trying to make a difference. Side note: before asking for help have a MVP (minimum viable product) so that they see your potential vision rather than just words with no concept behind them.

3) Realize that in order to create a wide scale change it takes more than just you. "Magnificent" projects are done by groups of people. When speaking about *Just Yell Fire* as the spokesperson, I often say "we did this" and "we did that" because the global impact of *Just Yell Fire* would not have happened without the help of everyone involved, from people who ran errands on set, to our graphics people, to our trainers. Everyone is a part of the success and you must never forget that. The success of your project is because of everyone who helps you on your journey to achieve your dream.

4) See what leaders in your industry are doing, what works and what does not, as well as what they are lacking. Combine the good with what's lacking and that is where you'll find your niche.

5) Never give up. You will have to make a lot of calls and perhaps experience a lot of rejection but in the end, if you continue to put your project out there you will connect with the right people who will steer you in the right direction. Never underestimate where it will happen either. Everyone has something to teach you, good and bad, so put yourself

out there and you'll be able to grow and have your idea grow quickly.

6) Never forget that it is not about you, it is about the cause. The minute your focus changes to something more self-serving, you may as well quit, because it becomes very transparent and will cause more damage to a cause than good.

www.justyellfire.com

Dani Bowman

I'm an 18-year-old individual with autism and I love animation, illustration and creating fun entertainment for children of all ages. I founded my company called **Power Light Animation Studios** at age 11 and I have been working professionally since age 14, partnering with Joey Travolta and teaching animation to others with autism at his summer camp program. I have illustrated 5 books and premiered three animated short films, "Mr. Raindrop" and "The Namazu" at Comic-Con in San Diego in 2012, and "Hannah Lost Her Smile" in 2013.

"Mr. Raindrop" is a story about a drop of water that wishes to be a rain drop and his wish comes true. It premiered at Wonder-Con 2012 in Anaheim and was also screened at Comic-Con in San Diego. The film was accepted for the New Orleans Children's Film Festival as well as the Los Angeles International Children's Film Festival at the LA County Museum of Art and AniMazSpot in the fall of 2012. It was also as awarded Best Student Animation Short by the Interntional Family Festival in 2013.

Magnificent Kids!

The second short, "The Namazu" premiered at Comic-Con 2012 and features the voice of the talented Tom Kenny (the voice of Sponge Bob Square Pants) as both the Narrator and The Namazu, Stella Ritter as Dani, with music written and performed by Lauren Dair Owens (the young Zoe Deschanel on Fox's "New Girl") and Will Clay.

Finally, "Hannah Lost Her Smile" premiered at Comic-Con 2013 and features the vocal talents of Stella Ritter as Hannah. In this heartwarming story, young Hannah wakes up to find that she has lost her smile and strives to get it back. It won Best Animated Short in 2013 at the Outside the Box Film Festival.

My life story was recently featured by RethinkingAutism.com in the animated video "Believe It: The Dani Bowman Story". "Believe it", produced by **Powerlight Studios** and RethinkingAutism.com, is an inspirational video that tells the story of the founding of **Powerlight Studios** and was produced with the assistance of autistic storyboard artist Justin Canha, autistic singer and songwriter Talina Toscano, voiced by Dani Bowman with voice over production and tag line by autistic actress Tammy Klein. You can see the video in the animations section of my website.

I speak frequently about my work and autism with the goal of changing the world's perception of autism and I hope to inspire others to follow their dreams. I have spoken at my high school, the Barnesdale Theater in Hollywood, Southern California Gas Company, Cal-TOSH, California Avocado Festival in Carpinteria, Orange County Festival of Children's Books, the Rotary Club in Auburn Hills, Michigan, and at Girltopia, a meeting of over 12,000 Girl Scouts at Staples Center in Los Angeles. I am also a contributing member of 'Awareness in a Box', which creates inclusionary events for the typical and special needs communities. I also participate in the Autism Community by serving as a committee member for 'Walk Now For Autism Speaks' in Los Angeles, which is one of the largest walks in the country. More information about my public appearances can be found in the speaking section of my website.

In 2010, I was honored for my contributions to the autistic community and for my animation talent by ANCA Naturally Autistic in Vancouver, BC, Canada. I was asked to host the 2011 edition of the awards, taught a workshop during the awards weekend, and was also named one of the 2012 International Ambassadors by ANCA, a role that Temple Grandin herself played for ANCA in 2011. The autism conference organizer, Future Horizons, honored me with their annual Temple Grandin Award for my work in autism advocacy and mentoring others with autism. Also my artwork is included in the book "Art of Autism" by Debra Hosseini.

To acknowledge my campaign against bullying, I was honored with the Golden Goody Award on April 20th, 2012 at the Deutsch Advertising Agency in Los Angeles. The award was presented by Teen Actor Lauren Dair Owens, who plays the young Zooey Deschanel on Fox channel's "New Girl". Actors and activists were there to support me and my anti-bully messages, including Zach Callison (Prince James in Disney's Sofia the First), Stella Ritter (Are You Smarter than a 5th Grader?), Kevin Sean Michaels (Producer, who works with Academy Award Nominee Bill Plympton), Amy Yasback (John Ritter's widow who runs the John Ritter Foundation,) Leeann Tweeden (Nascar Nation), Dana Commandatore and Actor Michael Broderick (Rethinking Autism Co-Founders and parents of an autistic son).

In celebration of Autism Acceptance Month, I donated an iPad that I had won in an animation contest and arranged fund raisers to raise money for two additional iPads to be given to non-verbal children with Autism Spectrum Disorder. I also arranged for iPad apps to be donated by Extra Special Kids, an iPad developer. The Goody Awards also donated an iPad in my name for being honored with a Golden Goody.

I work closely with Joey Travolta and his Inclusion Films group, which has the mission of teaching practical and employability skills to members of the special needs community. I have instructed at both the Burbank and Bakersfield campuses of the Inclusion Films program, where students are prepared for work in film and entertainment. I have animated titles for class projects such as "Mia's

Magnificent Kids!

Make-Up Corner", an anti-bullying campaign featured on CBS2 in Los Angeles, and "The Cave" by Arrest My Sister, a band fronted by Scott Siegel, who also has autism and is a student at Inclusion Films.

During the summers of 2011-2013, I took **Powerlight Studios** on the road, teaching animation to kids with autism at Joey Travolta's summer camp and at OCALI in Columbus, OH. Due to my close working relationship with Toon Boom Animation, a major animation software provider, Toon Boom supported me to travel to camps in Jacksonville, FL, Edgewood Cliffs, NJ, and Detroit, MI. At the camps, I taught animation to over 400 kids with autism, inspiring others on the spectrum to follow their dreams as well. This fall I will be mentoring some camp students, helping them develop their animation projects. For more information about the camps, please see http://www.inclusionfilms.com/camps/

Employing others with ASD has been a dream of mine since founding **Powerlight Studios** at age 11. With the expansion of commercial work requests, I am now in a position to hire others to help with my projects. I am now training my first employee in Los Angeles, 18 year old Conner Walsh, and I am mentoring two others with autism, 16 year old Luke Virgin a student from the Detroit OU Cares Camp, and Justin Canha, a 22 year old artist featured in the New York Times, http://www.nytimes.com/2011/09/18/us/autistic-and-seeking-a-place-in-an-adult-world.html?_r=1&hpw who also has a close working relationship with autistic musicians Scott Siegel, Nick Guzman and Talina Toscano.

I have been working professionally as an animator and illustrator since age 14, starting with the music video "The Cave" for the band Arrest My Sister produced by Joey Travolta. Since then, I have illustrated two anti-bullying books for Picalata Press with the second title "Richie and Goliath" being carried at Barnes and Noble. I have illustrated for the book "Rajalika Speak" about a talking horse, and "Really, Really" an autism awareness picture book written by published autistic poet and writer Gretchen Leary.

I have also won several awards for the autism awareness short "Eeya's Story" and I have completed several commercial projects including titles for "Power 1490, the Birth and Death of a Hip-Hop Radio Station in Tuscon, AZ", and "Vegan with Joy", a vegan cooking show available on iTunes. I also animated the opening titles for "Under the Dog House", a web series produced by Bruce Nachsin that has over 80,000 hits on Youtube, see http://underthedoghouse.com/ .

My first series was "Gemstar & Friends" (inspired by "Sonic Says") written at age 11, followed by "The Adventures of Captain Yuron" about a character who accidentally falls through a black hole and ends up in a new world where he defends his new friends from the pesky villain Malaria and his 16 minions. I now have 8 original series that I write, animate, voice, and score, ranging from Space Aliens in "Fleen the Alien" to a whole undersea world in "Hydro the Mako". While I continue to write scripts for my own properties, I have recently had to focus on my growing backlog of commercial animation for others.

I recently spent a week in Columbus, OH, teaching animation to individuals with Autism at OCALI, the Ohio Center for Autism and Low Incidence, as part of OCALI's mission to provide employability skills to individuals on the autism spectrum. I will expand the program with OCALI for 2013, incorporating live action film production as well.

In January 2012, Janro Imaging Laboratories selected me to be one of three sponsored artists for their new Freehand Stereoscopic Animation System, SANDDE providing equipment and technology to *Powerlight Studios*. The first project to utilize SANDDE is "Hanna Lost her Smile" voiced by Stella Ritter, a friend of mine and the youngest daughter of actor John Ritter, and story boarded by fellow autistic artist Justin Cahna.

I also continue to develop my skills and talents. I have taken Saturday High classes at Art Center School of Design in Pasadena and during the summer of 2011 I attended Open Studio with the Chair of the Animation Department at Woodbury University in Burbank, a class normally attended by Sophomores and Juniors in college. In 2012, I was selected as one of 16 Frieberg Fellows

Magnificent Kids!

scholars to attend Loyola Marymount University's Summer Creative Workshop. During the two week resident program, the 16 fellows produced two live action and two animated short films from script to screening.

I have been featured on HLN, CBS2 Los Angeles, ABC7 Los Angeles, Channel 3 in Orange County and in my local and school newspapers. You can see current media links at: http://www.powerlight-studios.com/Media

Achievements and awards include:
- Participation in the "AGI"
- La Canada, CA PTA "Reflections" 2013, film, 3rd place and art, 2nd place
- "Genius of Autism" McCarton Foundation Honoree, October 29th, 2012, New York, NY
- Loyola Marymount University, Fieberg Fellow 2012, Summer Creative Workshop
- SparkAction.com California Youth Innovation Award for Autism Employment June 2012
- Amazing Kid for May 2012, "Danielle Bowman, Amazing Animator!"
- New Horizon's "Temple Grandin Award" for Community Service, April 2012
- "The Golden Goody" for Social Good-Anti Bullying Campaigns, April 2012
- La Canada, CA PTA "Reflections" 2012, film, 2nd place.
- ToonBoom Animation, FlipBoom Valentine's Day Animation Contest
- La Canada, CA PTA "Reflections" 2011, film, 2nd place.
- "Diversity", La Canada High School, speaking, 1st Place
- VSA All Kids Can 2011, print "Imagination" representing the State of California
- ANCA Naturally Autistic, Outstanding Animator, Worldwide 2010
- Arts for Autism/Javamo Coffee, "Captain Coco" Packaging Design 2010

My company, **Powerlight Studios**, has several collaborative programs with like-minded organizations that work to develop, support and nurture others on the Autism Spectrum. Our goal is to find and celebrate others and their skills and talents. These programs showcase the various talents of people on the spectrum through art exhibits, showcases, readings, films and entertainment events. I aspire to be the Temple Grandin of my generation, working to change the world's perception of autism and demonstrating all of the special abilities that people with autism have, while striving for acceptance and integration within society as well as employing others with an Autism Spectrum Disorder at my company **Power Light Animation Studios**.

What does the word 'magnificent' mean to you?

To me, magnificent means that I have a great talent in animation. I started my animation company at a young age, 14 years old. I partnered with Joey Travolta's inclusion Film to animate my friend's first musical called "The Cave", did an animation segment called "Super Heroes only exist in Cartoons" for the Anti-Bullying PSA, and animated my first short film "Eeya's Story". I also illustrated and published the books "Danny & Goliath, "Richie & Goliath", "Rajalika Speak", and "Really Really Like Me". I screened 3 animated shorts "Mr. Raindrop", "The Namazu" and "Hannah Lost Her Smile" at San Diego Comic-Con. I even teach animation with Joey Travolta's Inclusion Film Camps in Jacksonvile FL with FilmLab & HEAL, Edgewood NJ with Marble Jam Kids, Detroit MI with OUcares, San Diego CA with COX & Act Today and Lafayette CA with Futures Explored; plus I teach animation independently at Columbus Ohio with OCALI.

What do you give to the world?

I give the world hope and inspiration for people on the autism spectrum, so they will follow their dreams. I have befriended, mentored, and helped people all around country and over the past three years, I have taught about 600 people.

Why is this important to you?

It's important to me because it improves my ability to work with others, but more importantly, I help other kids on the autism spectrum develop their social skills and self confidence.

Why did you choose the project/idea that you did?

I chose this idea because I love animation and wanted to have a career in animation since I was 11 years old. A career helps me to earn money to pay for college and investments, while inspiring others on the autism spectrum to follow their dreams too. I aim to change the world's perception of autism. ***Power Light Animation Studios*** is where I do animation and tell creative stories. It's a job that I love.

How old were you when you began your project?

I started ***Power Light Animation Studios*** when I was 11 years old, but I officially launched it at age 14.

How did you go about getting it started?

When I was 11, I found out that there is a person who started his company at age 17. His name is Satoshi Tariji, the Co-Creator of

Pokémon who is diagnosed with Asperger's syndrome, a form of autism. So I launched my animation company at age 14 to beat his record.

Who is your project benefiting, and how?

Powerlight Studios benefits me to become completely self sufficient, but I'm also inspiring others who are on the autism spectrum like me.

Who were the key people that supported you, and how?

The people that supported me are my Aunt Sandy, Uncle Patrick, Joey Travolta, Dori Littell-Herrick and Sondra Williams. My Aunt teaches me all about the life skills that will help me get through life. My uncle bought me a copy of Toon Boom Studio, which helps me make my animation company successful. Joey Travolta takes me to his film camps around the country to teach animation to students on the autism spectrum. Dori from Woodbury University taught me all about the animation principles and the basics of a storyboard. Sondra Williams believes in me and she invites me to Ohio to teach animation at OCALI.

How much financial assistance did you have, and from whom?

My uncle originally gave me some money for financial help, but now I'm self-funded.

How will you keep your project going into the future?

I will continue on my education, plus I will have my own animation studio building where I will employ people on the autism spectrum to create television series, films, video games, etc.

How have your peers responded to you setting up the project, and do they (or can they) get involved in any way?

My peers are positively surprised and inspired by me. Some ask their parents if they can meet me, some 'friend request me' on social networks, some show me to the younger generations and others have wanted to work with me by showing me their talents on storyboards, musical scores, voice acting, character & background design, screenwriting, directing, film editing and much more.

Do you see yourself as ordinary or extraordinary?

I see myself as extraordinary, because my autism gives me the ability to create amazing stories.

What is the most important thing to you?

The most important thing about me is my life with autism and that I didn't let autism hold me back. When I was about 2 years old, I was in my own little world and my parents couldn't reach me. Then a year later, I was first diagnosed with autism. I didn't speak until the age of 5, the same age when I started drawing. I began to create my own books and this was my first talent. I did not have support until I moved to my Aunt Sandy and Uncle Patrick's house after 6th grade at age 11. I didn't understand what autism was until I discovered the meaning on the Internet. While running *Power Light Animation Studios*, I also graduated from High School with a diploma, a 4.0 GPA, and I've been a member of the National Honors Society. So that means, never let your handicap hold you back, and that's the most important message.

What are your strengths?

My strengths are animation, science, screenwriting, voice acting, character & background design, directing and film editing, just to name a few!

What are your weaknesses?

My worst weaknesses are grammar, vocabulary and a lack of focus. It affects my writing and my speech so I get stuck sometimes when I'm talking. I have to get over my weakness by improving my grammar and vocabulary.

Does your project require you to focus on your strengths?

Yes it does, not only for my artistic skills, but also for the business side of my animation company. To work on the business side, I will have to transfer from GCC to Woodbury University to study business.

Who is your greatest role model and why?

I have so many great role models such as John Lasseter, The Fothergil brothers of Strange Flavour ltd., Temple Grandin, Satoshi Tariji, Shigeru Miyamoto and Masashiro Sankurai among others. Satoshi Tariji, the creator of Pokémon, is on the autism spectrum like me and has inspired me to create my own series including "The Captain Yuron" series. John Lasseter has given me inspiration to remember that the best animation tells a great story.

Of all the people in the world, who inspires you the most?

The person who inspires me the most is Temple Grandin. She is a person on the autism spectrum who inspires me to change the world's perception of autism. She also inspires me because she is capable of taking care of herself and is best known for saying, "We are autistic, not less".

How/where/why did you learn to care globally?

I care globally because many parents find that having a child with autism is devastating and they think their child will have a difficult life. 1 in 88 children will be diagnosed with autism, in the US 500,000 individuals with autism will turn 18 this year, and about 89% of adults with autism will not be in the workforce (65% in poverty, 15% unemployed, 9% underemployed).

If you could change one thing in the world, what would it be?

I'm here to change the world's perception of autism and to demonstrate all of the special abilities that people with autism have, while striving for acceptance and integration within society.

What do you think are the ingredients for success?

For success, you must have talent, academics, focus, time and you must work hard. If you have all 5 together, it will make your life easier.

What is your global vision?

In my vision, people on the autism spectrum are capable and self-supporting, doing what they really love, and socially accepted by the whole world. I also want ***Power Light Animation Studios*** to be a huge building, so I can employ many people with special needs especially the ones on the autism spectrum.

What would be your message to the world?

Focus on your ability, not your disability, no matter where on the spectrum you are! Also always never give up and follow your dreams, work for something you love.

If other kids wanted to start up their own magnificent project, what advice would you give them and what steps would you suggest they take?

If you want to start your project, you're never too young! All you have to do is you must get help from your parents and/or your peers. Keep working as hard as possible, no matter how hard it seems, it will lead you to success.

www.powerlight-studios.com

"Every kid is one caring adult
away from being a success."
~ Josh Shipp

Daniel & William Clarke

Daniel:

Hi, I'm Daniel Clarke. In 2006 at the age of 10, I began my quest to save the orangutans and their habitat in Borneo. I was a big fan of the Crocodile Hunter, Steve Irwin, and ironically his death inspired me to save the orangutans. I asked Mum,
'Who is going to save the orangutans now?'
and then straight away I said,
'I will save them,'
and that was the beginning of our quest.

A series of events and chance meetings occurred over the next 2 years and in 2008 I found myself in Borneo with my family, travelling for seven days through the jungle to get to the orangutans. This seven day trek was not easy as I have cerebral palsy and spend almost all of my time in a wheelchair. With help from the locals, who carried me in my wheelchair over the rugged terrain, we came around a corner in the jungle and saw our first orangutan. It was amazing!

After travelling to Borneo, my brother William and I wrote our book, *'Tears In The Jungle'*. We wanted to let other kids around the world know about the orangutans and that they are critically endangered. We knew that not everyone would have the opportunity to see the jungle for themselves so we wanted to give them the opportunity, through our book, to see what it was like and understand what is happening through our own travels. Our quest has also been featured on the TV program, 'Australian Story'.

William, who is two years younger than I am, joined me in my quest in 2009, and together we are raising a lot of funds and awareness for the orangutans. Our aim is to raise one million dollars to sponsor land that will remain a safe haven for orangutans. So far we have raised $708,000 and have sponsored 79,000 acres of land in Borneo.

When President Obama visited Australia in November 2012 I thought, 'Wouldn't it be great if President Obama was able to receive one of our books!' So I wrote a letter to the Ambassador for the United States of America, Jeffrey Bleich, asking if he could pass a copy on. Then in December we received a letter from Ambassador Bleich wishing us all the best and providing words of encouragement. It didn't provide any indication that our book had been passed on to the President during his visit but was very supportive nonetheless for which we were very appreciative.

Four months later, when Mum went to collect the mail from the post box just before collecting us from school, imagine her surprise when she was handed a brown paper envelope which read, 'United States of America – Official Business'.

Her heart skipped a beat...

She realised the letter had been postmarked from Canberra so she was pretty sure it was from Ambassador Bleich and thought it was a certificate, or photo, or something commemorating President Obama's visit to Australia in response to my letter. As the letter was addressed to me, Mum wanted to make sure that I was there when it was opened so she quickly jumped into the car and drove to the school.

At the school, Mum got me out of my wheelchair and sitting comfortably in the back seat of the car, William stood beside her at the side of the car while they opened the envelope together. She carefully opened the envelope and was shocked that inside was another brown paper envelope, except this time, on the outside of the envelope were the words, '**The White House, Washington DC – FIRST CLASS DO NOT BEND**'.

Mum and William looked at each other in disbelief.
Mum said,
'I cannot open this here, I have to get a letter opener.'
She asked me if I wanted to go home and open it but I said,
'No, let's go to the school office.'

Mum quickly unloaded the wheelchair, strapped me in and, with William in tow, headed off briskly to the school office. The school office was winding down at the end of the day and as we walked in, Mum asked the lady behind the desk if she had a letter opener. She casually said,
'Yes, we have one here… somewhere.'
Mum couldn't help herself and said,
'Daniel has received a letter from The White House!'
You should have seen everyone's faces!

In seconds, staff were rushing from all directions. There was a small crowd around us as Mum nervously opened the envelope and pulled the letter out for us to read first. Everyone had tears in their eyes. At the top of the letter was an embossed coat of arms of the United States of America. Underneath it, it said, 'The White House, Washington', and at the end of the letter was the original signature of The President of the United States.

The letter was simple, however one phrase stood out, "I look forward to working together to the benefit of our two nations, and to strengthening the bonds between our people".

Magnificent Kids!

William:

Our whole family was a fan of Steve Irwin and we were greatly saddened when he passed away back in September 2006. Daniel was particularly upset. Just before Steve died, Daniel watched a documentary by Kim Watkins, 'Saving Orangutans', and was really motivated by the issues the orangutans were facing, so when Steve passed away Daniel said to Mum and Dad,
'Who is going to be saving orangutans now that Steve Irwin has gone?'
Mum and Dad's response was,
'Well, you can save them if you want to?'

Daniel has cerebral palsy and most of the time is confined to a wheelchair. On the inside, Daniel was still an energetic 10 year old just trapped in a body that didn't perform as well as other people's.

In 2007, Daniel was approached by the Starlight Foundation who wanted to grant him a wish. We were delighted at the prospect, not just for Daniel but for our family as a whole. Ideas were rushing through our heads like, a trip to Disneyland, a new computer for Daniel, maybe even a new car to carry his wheelchair, etc. However, Mum and Dad made us realise this was Daniel's wish and we needed to give him the opportunity to make this decision himself. Mum and Dad talked to Daniel and me to explain about this wonderful opportunity and to talk through some of the many options that may be available to him.

Daniel listened to what they had to say and then said,
'I want to save the orangutans in Borneo.'
We were all shocked. Dad said,
'Are you sure?'
'What about a trip to Disneyland or a new car... for daddy?' Dad said in a pleading voice.
'No Dad, I want to save the orangutans in Borneo,' Daniel said.

Our next step was to call up The Starlight Foundation and advise them of the decision Daniel had made. The telephone conversation was certainly interesting…

'He wants to do what?'

After several days of digesting Daniel's request, Mum received a telephone call from The Starlight Foundation to advise that they had never had a child who wanted a selfless wish and they were really shocked. In fact, we were told they had boardroom meetings to discuss the impact of Daniel's wish and how touched they were. Although The Starlight Foundation tried hard to accommodate Daniel's wish, we ended up settling on a compromise - a trip to Australia Zoo, which in itself was wonderful.

Daniel was still determined to save orangutans and Mum and Dad realised that his heart's desire had not been met. They talked with him and found a way for him to make a difference. We located the website of The Orangutan Project (TOP) which offered a service that allowed people to adopt an orangutan for just $55 per year. So, using his own money, Daniel adopted an orangutan. After a while, Daniel started talking with some of his friends and in a short time we realised there were quite a few people who were adopting an orangutan in Daniel's name.

Daniel then said,
'I'm going to raise $10,000 to save the orangutan,' and spoke to the Principal of his school and designed an 'orang-a-thon' which is a dua-thalon event for which the children at the school gain sponsorship for every lap they complete either on foot or on a bike. The event raised a massive $5,200 and Daniel was on his way.

Dad then contacted TOP (The Orangutan Project) and let them know that he was Daniel's dad and asked if they were getting any orangutan adoptions that mentioned 'Daniel Clarke'.
The response was,
'I am so pleased you made contact, in fact we have.'

It wasn't long after that we received a phone call from TOP advising they would like to offer Daniel the title of National Children's Ambassador for the Australian Orangutan Project for all of the fund raising and awareness raised for the plight of the orangutan. It is a title which has since generated a huge amount of media interest.

In May, 2008, The Starlight Foundation asked our family if we would like to see a Rugby Union Football match between the Wallabies and Wales at our local stadium and if they won their game, would we like to meet the Wallabies in the dressing room after the match? The answer was obviously 'yes'! Luckily, the Wallabies won their match and we were escorted down to the dressing room to meet them and congratulate them on a job well done. Daniel was in his wheelchair when, to our surprise, we realised that we were standing right next to our Prime Minister Honourable John Howard.

Daniel, realising he had a great opportunity, asked Mum, 'Can I tell Mr Howard what I am trying to do with the Orangutan?' Mum agreed. Dad introduced himself and all of us to Mr Howard, who was very nice and friendly.

The Prime Minister knelt down beside Daniel while he slowly explained to him about his quest to Save the Orangutan of Borneo and Sumatra. Mr Howard listened attentively. On standing up, Mr Howard thanked Daniel for sharing his quest with him and turned to Dad to ask if he had a business card. Dad passed Mr Howard a business card and wrote on the back, 'Daniel, orangutan, $10,000'. Mr Howard said,
'I can't promise anything, but I will be in touch.'

It was only six weeks later when we received a letter from our Prime Minister advising that after meeting Daniel he was pledging $500,000 over four years to an American Non-Government Organisation to help save the orangutan. Daniel was thrilled, but that was only the start.

The Prime Minister also visited Daniel at our home in Sydney, and that was certainly one of Daniel's most memorable experiences. The rest of us were pretty excited too!

Daniel & William:

We were invited to attend INXS's last performance on their Coast to Coast tour out at Penrith Panthers. It was the first time we had ever been to a rock concert so we knew we were going to have a great night. After receiving a wonderful video message of support from INXS earlier in the year, we were thrilled to receive an invitation to come along before the show and meet all the guys in person. We gave each of the band members a toy orangutan to say thanks for their support and video message. The guys loved them.

Half way through the concert Tim Farriss took the microphone to announce that the next song was 'new' and 'inspired by Daniel and William Clarke and their work to save the orangutans'. We were very shocked but our smiles went from ear to ear. We were thrilled to think our book had inspired a legendary rock band to write a song. We LOVED it as it had a real jungle beat to it. The song is called, 'Tears in the Rain'.

We also have many high profile celebrity supporters who have their hearts and minds in the right place. Megan Gale, Joel Madden, Seal, Bear Grylls, Dick Smith and Giaan Rooney are just a few. You can see the full list on our 'Celebrity Supporters' page on our website.

Magnificent Kids!

What does the word 'magnificent' mean to you?

Daniel: I would use the word 'Magnificent' to describe the orangutans because the word conjures up perceptions of majestic animals, beautiful creatures that are so close to humans, living in one of the most idyllic habitats on our planet.

William: 'Magnificent' to me is something that is considered very special.

What do you give to the world?

Daniel: Even with my disability, I hope that I give inspiration to many kids around Australia and the world to know that nothing is impossible and that everyone can make a difference and to follow your dreams.

William: I hope my actions inspire the next generation to let them know that whatever actions they take, for whatever goals they set themselves, they will make a huge difference in our world.

Why is this important to you?

Daniel: It's important to me as I am following my dreams and my passion and if I can do it, even with a disability, anyone can make a difference. Don't let anyone tell you 'you can't' or, 'it's impossible', because it doesn't matter who you are or where you come from, we can all make a difference.

William: I believe it's our generation who will fix the problems that generations before us have set in motion. Dan and I hope to inspire our generation to know that, even as kids, we have the power to make a huge difference to our world.

Why did you choose the project/idea that you did?

Daniel: It all started when I was four years old. I always watched 'The Crocodile Hunter', which were documentaries made by Steve

Irwin. The documentary he made about the orangutans really affected me. I watched the orangutan episode over and over. I loved the interaction between Steve and the orangutans and his passion for saving wildlife inspired me. When Steve died suddenly in 2006, I knew I had to 'step-up' and do something to save the orangutans.

William: After seeing the work that Dan was doing and the impact that it was having on people I thought, by joining Dan in his quest, the two of us could make a much bigger difference than either one of us could do alone.

How old were you when you began your project?

Daniel: I started when I was 10 with a goal to raise $10,000 and then our family travelled to Borneo when I was 12 and William was 10. It was then, after our trip, we both talked about writing a book about our experiences, which included photographs that we had taken on the trip.

How did you go about getting it started?

Daniel: I first started by adopting an orangutan called 'Lydia' through The Orangutan Project. Then I did a school project about the orangutans and got all my friends to adopt an orangutan. I then talked with my school principal about doing an 'orang-a-thon' (where every student was sponsored per lap, around the school oval, for walking or running for 20 minutes and then cycling around the oval for 20 minutes.) We were able to raise $5,200 from that one event and our school only had 360 students. I was so inspired that I decided to take my quest to a whole new level. I thought to myself, 'Imagine what I could do outside of school,' and our quest began.

In 2007 I had a chance meeting with the Australian Prime Minister the Honourable John Howard. After meeting him, and explaining to him about my quest, he was so inspired that his government pledged $500,000 over four years to help save the orangutans. Now I knew I could really make a difference so I began writing letters to everyone I could think of who was famous, to let them know about the orangutans and to ask for their support. Many did not reply but occasionally I received a reply like the one from Barack Obama and INXS, and that was truly amazing.

Who is your project benefiting, and how?

Daniel: Our project is benefitting the orangutans of Borneo and Sumatra in Indonesia because we are sponsoring land and adopting orangutans. So far we have sponsored 79,600 acres of land and adopted 92 orangutans. Also through our school talks we are spreading our message about the orangutans to create greater awareness of the situation they face as they will become extinct in the wild in less than 10 years.

William: The more that people are aware of the orangutan situation, the more they want to help. It is sad to think that our generation may be the last generation to see them roaming free in the wild.

Who were the key people that supported you, and how?

Daniel & William:
1. Our Mum and Dad are our biggest supporters.
2. The Honourable Prime Minister John Howard and his government at the time, as they pledged $500,000
3. There are several key business people who have supported us in our quest including, Australian Adventurer and Entrepreneur Dick Smith AO, as he wrote the forward to our book.
4. Many other Australian and International celebrities have pledged their support (Celebrity Supporters page - http://tearsinthejungle.com/in-the-media/celebrity-supporters/)

How much financial assistance did you have, and from whom?

Daniel & William: Our trip to Borneo in 2008 was paid for by an anonymous donor (we still don't know who the generous person was who changed our lives). Actually, we have done everything else on our own, even self-publishing our book as no publisher thought that our book would be successful as we were kids and first time authors. With our sales now in excess of 5,000 books, our book is being listed on the Premier's Reading Challenge for NSW and Victoria and is being used in schools and universities around Australia and overseas. Our book is considered to be in the 'Best- Seller' category in Australia.

How will you keep your project going into the future?

Daniel: William and I will keep on talking to schools around Australia to spread our message. We also hope to go back to Borneo and write a second book that is an update on what is happening in Borneo. The book will be about showing everyone the progress and the change that we are making over in Borneo through everyone's support. There are great things happening to save the orangutans such as land being bought by Orangutan Foundation International (OFI) through their Rawa Kuno Legacy Forest which is patrolled by rangers. As a result, there is now a safe area for orangutans to be released.

How have your peers responded to you setting up the project, and do they (or can they) get involved in any way?

Daniel & William: Our friends have been really supportive to us throughout our quest. They are always there to help us when we do our presentations at corporate functions and they help us to pack books and answer phone calls. Our friends really keep us down to earth and keep us focussed on the task at hand. After the school talks we receive many requests and emails asking how the students can help. We always suggest they can help by holding 'mufti-days' where everyone wears the colour orange for a gold coin donation, to hold a cake stall or just to adopt their own orangutan or to get the whole class to adopt an orangutan. All the money raised goes directly to The Orangutan Project (TOP), Borneo Orangutan Survival (BOS) or Orangutan Foundation International Australia (OFI) which are the main charities we support.

Do you see yourself as ordinary or extraordinary?

Daniel: We have never once seen ourselves as extraordinary as we believe that anyone can make a difference by following their passion, whatever that may be, to make our world a better place.

William: We are just two brothers from Sydney Australia, doing what we believe is right and trying to make a difference.

What is the most important thing to you?

Daniel: Knowing that we are making a difference, not only in Borneo but around the world. We only have one planet and we really need to look after it. I also hope that I inspire other people with disabilities to let them know that you can still achieve anything if you set your mind to it. Don't let people say, 'You can't.' We all have a voice to be heard.

William: Our actions are not only saving the orangutans, we are helping the world and also inspiring the next generation to make a difference and to make our world a better place than it is at the moment.

What are your strengths?

Daniel: My strengths are determination and persistence. I try to see things through to the end, never give up, follow my passion and my dreams. My attitude of never giving up is about working with others towards a common goal and always being happy and always seeing the positive side of everything.

William: I have gained experience in public speaking as now Daniel and I have spoken to over 40 schools and 19,000 students. I have persistence and determination to see our quest to the point where the future of the orangutans is no longer threatened by mankind.

What are your weaknesses?

Daniel: My weakness is organisation, but I am working on it!!

William: Nerves, I always get nervous before our talks but I am trying to conquer that. The more we do the better I get.

Does your project require you to focus on your strengths?

Daniel: Yes, because we have had to develop our strengths through what we do and then we use these strengths to do what we do, even better!

Who is your greatest role model and why?

Daniel: Steve Irwin. As he had such a passion for wildlife and he spoke with that passion everywhere he went. He spoke with passion in his documentaries. He never gave any thought to what people thought of him. He kept powering on and doing what he loved, knowing that he was making a difference. As Steve Irwin said, 'Be passionate and enthusiastic in the direction that you choose in life and you will be a winner!'

Of all the people in the world, who inspires you the most?

Daniel: The Honourable John Howard, because seeing what he was able to achieve in his term as Prime Minster, and meeting him, has inspired me to study environmental law and then go into politics as I believe this is where I can make a difference on a global scale.

William: My brother Daniel. Although he has a physical disability (cerebral palsy) and has so many obstacles in his path, he shows such determination and passion to achieve his goals. With his quick wit and humour, his compassionate outlook on life and empathy for others, it is hard not to be inspired by him. Dan makes me strive to achieve my best in everything I do. His passion is infectious and to be a part of this quest with him has been an amazing experience.

How/where/why did you learn to care globally?

Daniel: Through Steve Irwin. We knew we could care globally as he travelled around the world to create awareness of all animals that are endangered. He always believed that if people could relate to animals in some way, they would be more willing to help them and that's what we believe in our quest. I think this is why our book has been so successful as it shows the interaction of the orangutans with William and myself. The photos in our book show how intelligent the orangutans are, the emotions they can share with us and how you can communicate between species without using spoken words.

If you could change one thing in the world, what would it be?

Daniel: I would change the economy, as currently it is based on continual growth and is a key factor for why mankind is damaging our earth. What we need is a system that is based on **sustainable growth** so that we don't have to destroy the environment. We can still survive as a human race in balance with nature.

What do you think are the ingredients for success?

Daniel: Passion. You have to have passion otherwise you won't know what you are striving to achieve. If you love what you do, you will never work a day in your life because every day is enjoyable.

William: Goal setting. It's important to remember to set yourself small goals to begin with, and these will give you direction for your end goal. Then you can see where you are going, where you are and what you have already achieved.

What is your global vision?

Daniel: That humans would put a greater emphasis on environmental issues including habitats and the importance of maintaining them, as we all need them to survive as a human race.

We only have one planet and we need to look after it for future generations.

William: That the world could live in harmony with our environment and that all animals could live in peace in their own natural habitat whether that be the deserts, the jungles or the oceans.

What would be your message to the world?

Daniel & William:

Our message to the world is;

> Our world is like a home. Everyone who lives in that home doesn't want to destroy it because they need to live there; they need that home for survival. It is the same for Earth. Humans are the occupants of Earth. This is our only home and we don't want to make it a filthy place, or destroy it to the point that it is too late to fix. We need to act now, while we have time. To have our home, Earth, in a better state in years to come, to be able to sustain humanity and all the creatures that also call Earth home.
>
> We can all make a difference, and it doesn't matter how big or small the actions are that you take. If everyone did one small thing, imagine what could be achieved if 7 billion people decided to take action?

If other kids wanted to start up their own magnificent project, what advice would you give them and what steps would you suggest they take?

Daniel & William:
The orangutans are not the only cause out there. There are many other causes and if you believe in one that is worth fighting for, fight

for it. Don't let anyone tell you, 'You can't do it,' or that, 'It is impossible,' because **nothing is impossible**. Remember, no matter who you are, or where you come from, we can all make a difference in our world. Whether it is an environmental issue or an animal that needs help, first go and find out about it, google it, find it on the web, find people in your area that you can help and volunteer and get to know all about it, then start involving your friends and family. Get your local schools to know about your cause and get your local newspapers involved. Do anything that helps you to get your message out there and create awareness. You will be amazed how quickly this can snowball into something big, as this is what happened to us.

www.TearsInTheJungle.com

Jack Andraka

When a close family friend passed away from pancreatic cancer, I didn't even know what a pancreas was, much less pancreatic cancer, so I turned to the place where any teenager goes for information - the Internet. Wikipedia and Google became my teachers while I learned everything I could about pancreatic cancer and methods of detection. What I discovered shocked me. Over 85% of pancreatic cancer patients are diagnosed late, when a person has less than a 2% chance of survival. I asked myself why we are so bad at detecting pancreatic cancer. After researching, I learned that our modern method is a 60 year old test that can cost over $800 and it misses more than 30% of cancers. I knew there had to be a better way!

So, armed with my teenage optimism, I started trolling through the Internet and found an interesting article on single walled carbon nanotubes. These little tubes of carbon are like the super heroes of material science: they are smaller than a strand of hair and have amazing electrical properties. I smuggled the article into my high school biology class and was reading it under my desk while my teacher lectured us on antibodies. Then an idea hit me! What if I combined what I was reading about (single walled carbon nanotubes) with what I was supposed to be learning about (antibodies) and came up with a way to detect pancreatic cancer?

Magnificent Kids!

Of course my idea had a million holes in it, but over the summer I patched up most of them and worked on my experimental design. Finally, I sent emails to 200 professors in my area who were studying anything to do with pancreatic cancer. I included my design, a materials list, budget, timeline and then I sat back and waited for the acceptances to roll in. I received 199 rejections and one 'maybe' from Dr Maitra of Johns Hopkins. I was interviewed by him, was given a small lab space and I went to work. Of course I had many setbacks and even some tears as I broke tubes of cell cultures that I had spent weeks growing, and struggled with the Western Blot. But after working nights, weekends and holidays I finally came up with a small paper strip the size of a diabetic test strip that can detect mesothelin, a biomarker for pancreatic cancer, with excellent sensitivity and specificity.

As a result of my research, I have been awarded many monetary prizes, honors and awards, and I've been named Top Young Scientist in Popular Science Magazine. I have received the Smithsonian American Ingenuity Award recognizing me as one of the most innovative individuals working in America today. Award winning documentaries featuring me include "You Don't Know Jack", "Just Jack", "ThinkR", and "A Day Without Cancer".

I have been featured in magazines including Time, Oprah, Forbes, Science News, Wired, Popular Science, Psychology Today, The Scientist, Discover Magazine, Scholastic, International Business times and many more both national and international. Newspaper articles include The New York Times, The Independent, The Daily Mail, The Examiner, The Times of India, Huffington Post, The Washington Post, Wall Street Journal, and other newspapers from around the world.

My TV appearances include 60 Minutes, CNN, BBC, The Colbert Report, Al Jazeera, World News Tonight with Diane Sawyer, CBS, ABC, FOX, CBC Canada, The View, The Today Show, The Doctors Show and others.

I have also appeared in books, on radio programs, blogs, and science panels. My speaking engagements have taken me all over the world including Greece, Spain, Australia, England, Switzerland, Mexico, Italy and Dubai, and I have presented at 16 TED and TEDx talks around the world, as well as at the White House Science Fair in 2013.

So if a 15 year old can use the Internet to create a sensor that detects pancreatic cancer, just imagine what you can do!

What does the word 'magnificent' mean to you?

For me, magnificent means going above and beyond expectations and helping to change the world.

What do you give to the world?

I create new diagnostic systems, particularly for cancer. I've worked on a novel paper sensor for pancreatic, ovarian, and lung cancer that costs 3 cents and takes 5 minutes to run. Currently, I'm working on the Tricorder X-Prize to develop a device that you scan over your skin to diagnose diseases instantly.

Why is this important to you?

This is important to me because I know that around the world millions of people die from undiagnosed or misdiagnosed diseases every year. For me a person's success is measured by their impact on humanity and how many lives they have touched rather than the amount of money they make. I had a personal reason to get into medical diagnostics, the passing of a close family friend from pancreatic cancer, however now my motivation is much broader.

Why did you choose the project/idea that you did?

I chose my project because a close family friend passed from the disease when I was 13. I soon realized that there was no standard diagnostic tool for the disease, and the current tests were outdated, expensive and inaccurate.

How old were you when you began your project?

I began the project when I was 14.

How did you go about getting it started?

I read a lot! I started with Wikipedia to start with because I needed basic information. Then I branched out to reading the bibliography on the site. Then I progressed to Google and then to reading lots of papers and journal articles. One day I smuggled one of these articles into my high school biology class and was reading it under my desk while my teacher lectured us on antibodies. Then an idea hit me! What if I combined what I was reading about (single walled carbon nanotubes) with what I was supposed to be learning about (antibodies) and came up with a way to detect pancreatic cancer?

Who is your project benefiting, and how?

This novel paper sensor is easy to make and very sensitive. I'm in talks with biotech companies to have it made more quickly and uniformly so it can go through clinical trials and get onto the market. This way it can serve as an inexpensive and rapid way of detecting cancer during annual physical exams.

Who were the key people that supported you, and how?

I had a lot of rejections before I was able to get into a lab. Dr Maitra, of Johns Hopkins University, agreed to be my mentor and give me access to his lab. My parents drove me to the lab and waited very long hours for me there.

How much financial assistance did you have, and from whom?

I was given about a $1,500 budget by Dr. Maitra's lab.

How will you keep your project going into the future?

I'm optimizing my components and also talking to companies so it can be commercially produced and marketed.

How have your peers responded to you setting up the project, and do they (or can they) get involved in any way?

People were worried that students at my school would be mean or jealous but they are pretty much all very happy and excited for me. I enjoy speaking to kids like me all around the world. So many of them write to me and share their dreams of solving big problems or share their frustrations about getting access to journal articles or lab space.

Do you see yourself as ordinary or extraordinary?

I'm a regular high school student who followed my curiosity and motivation, and with a lot of persistence and hard work, I found a sensor to detect pancreatic cancer.

What is the most important thing to you?

I want to contribute to and change the world for the better.

What are your strengths?

My strengths are that I'm stubborn, persistent, curious, hard working and I can communicate well.

What are your weaknesses?

My weakness is that I sometimes don't ask for help early enough.

Does your project require you to focus on your strengths?

My project was successful due to my strengths and I learned to ask for help early after making a few mistakes in the lab that required me to start over culturing cells.

Who is your greatest role model and why?

My greatest role model is Marie Curie because she won two Nobel prizes in an age when science was not really a career path many women were able to follow. She overcame many obstacles based on her gender and despite these, she accomplished so much.

Of all the people in the world, who inspires you the most?

Alan Turing inspired me because of the work he did that created the basis for the modern computer. It was a real thrill to see his papers when I visited Cambridge University in the UK.

How/where/why did you learn to care globally?

My family talks a lot about current events and history at the dinner table so we are all aware of our place as global citizens whose actions affect people in other parts of the world.

If you could change one thing in the world, what would it be?

I'm really interested in changing the way diseases are diagnosed and in improving them so people can live longer, healthier lives.

What do you think are the ingredients for success?

To read widely, experiment, persist and don't be afraid to fail.

What is your global vision?

I'd love everyone to have access to good health care and for kids like me to have open access to journals and the Internet so we can learn and innovate.

What would be your message to the world?

If a 15 year old, who didn't even know what a pancreas was, can create a sensor to detect pancreatic cancer using Google and Wikipedia, imagine what you can do!

If other kids wanted to start up their own magnificent project, what advice would you give them and what steps would you suggest they take?

I would recommend kids read a lot and think about what is important to them. They are going to spend a lot of time working on their projects so they need to really love what they are learning about and be highly motivated to learn as much as they can themselves. Don't expect people to spoon feed them but learn to hunt for information themselves and ask themselves questions and try to answer them.

www.jackandraka.net

Children are the living messages we send
to a time we will not see."
~ John W. Whitehead

Jessica Carscadden

My name is Jessica. I am 10 years old and I started the *We Care Bears Project*. I collect stuffed animals and give them to the police and fire departments to keep in their trunks for kids they meet who are scared or injured. I also donate them to Ronald McDonald House.

Let me tell you how it all started...

One day I was cleaning out my stuffed animals and a lot of them were almost new; many still had the tags on them. The fire department comes into contact with children at fires, auto accidents or EMT calls. The kids they meet are often scared. I thought that kids would be less scared if the firemen had stuffed animals to give the kids. We live across the street from a fire station so I thought about giving the local police and fire departments bags of stuffed animals to keep in the trunks of the cars and trucks so that they could give them to kids who may be scared or injured. The firemen didn't have any stuffed animals and they were happy that I donated mine.

Magnificent Kids!

I am only one girl and I took all of my animals to the fire department but I know that police officers also come into contact with kids who are scared, so I made a plan. I talked to the principal at my school, Dr. Newman, and asked him if I could ask the whole school to donate their stuffed animals. I thought maybe we would have enough stuffed animals to put some in the trunks of all the police cars at our local Sheriff's station and in the fire trucks and ambulances. Dr. Newman thought it was a good idea and that maybe if I presented it to the School Student Council, they could help me with the project.

I talked to the Sheriff's office and they have 6 cars, plus the fire station vehicles. I wanted to get stuffed animals into every vehicle. My initial goal was to put bags of stuffed animals into 10 vehicles, but so far I have been able to put them into 1,000 emergency response vehicles all over Southern California and Nevada. I have donated over 1,000 stuffed toys to the emergency services just in San Diego.

I was born in China but because I was born with medical issues including a cleft palate and lip, I was abandoned in an orphanage and put into a "dying room", which is a place where those who are not expected to survive live out the remainder of their lives. I was adopted by my family when I was 5 years old. When my Mom and Dad came to visit me and to work out my adoption arrangements, they gave me a teddy bear and that was the only toy I had in the whole 5 years I was in the orphanage, so I know how important it is to have something to hug. I have undergone many surgical procedures, one was to replace a missing jawbone and I still have several more operations to go, but that shouldn't stop me from trying to help other kids who might be scared.

I was featured in the "American Girl" magazine in July 2013. That was really cool! The US Bank is hosting a **We Care Bears** drive and for this year's 'Make a Difference Day' my classmates helped me put together 500 bags of bears to first responders. I received a Points of Light Award, Kohl's Cares Scholarship and 2012/2013 I served as "Historian" on the Student Council at my school. In 2012 I received the Unsung Hero Award and in 2013 I was featured in the San Diego Families magazine.

In October 2013 I was one of the ten winners of the inaugural Peace First Prize. This has really helped me to realize just how important **We Care Bears** is for the community and for making a difference. Peace First exists to create the next generation of peacemakers. They teach young people to work effectively with others to resolve conflicts, solve community problems, communicate ideas effectively and form positive social relationships. Also I recently found out that I am a 2013 National Make A Difference Day Honoree. I am going to Washington DC in April to accept this award and will meet Matt Lauer and Savannah Guthrie. I am so excited! When Mom found out Bon Jovi would be there too she couldn't stop squealing, but I don't really know why she did that.

In the city of San Diego, December 17, 2013 was declared "Jessica Carscadden Day". I was invited to speak to the entire City Council about my project. It was very special, but then I had to go back to school. I feel very honored to have received these awards and recognition and I take this responsibility very seriously.

What does the word 'magnificent' mean to you?

I think it means great.

Magnificent Kids!

What do you give to the world?

Well mostly my project is local, like San Diego, Los Angeles and Las Vegas. But I hope my project inspires other kids to start projects too.

Why is this important to you?

Because I can't change the world but I can help one child and that child can help one child and it can keep going like that and slowly the world can be a better place if everyone starts thinking about how they can help each other.

Why did you choose the project/idea that you did?

I was cleaning out my room and I had a lot of stuffed animals that I didn't love anymore. I live across the street from the fire department and I thought I could take my stuffed animals to them for kids they meet on calls. It grew from there.

How old were you when you began your project?

I was 8 years old.

How did you go about getting it started?

I just took my own stuffed animals but then I thought if I had stuffed animals that I didn't need, other kids might too. So I went to the principal of my school and asked if we could have a bear drive. I also asked other schools for their help and even local businesses have helped.

Who is your project benefiting, and how?

My project helps kids who are scared or injured by giving them a stuffed animal to "huggle". But it also helps the firemen and policemen too, because if a kid is calm it is easier for them to do their jobs.

Who were the key people that supported you, and how?

Mostly my parents by letting me do this as well as businesses like Chic-Fil-A, West Coast Fundraising, Shay Realtors and Storage West.

How much financial assistance did you have, and from whom?

My parents pay for almost everything. Some people donate 10 or 20 dollars. I was lucky that West Coast Fundraising used to donate all the bags but they can't do that anymore. Chic-Fil-A donated lots and lots of free food coupons for everyone who donated.

How will you keep your project going into the future?

I plan on having more bear drives and I would like to teach other kids how to do *We Care Bears* where they live.

How have your peers responded to you setting up the project, and do they (or can they) get involved in any way?

My friends think my project is great because they ALL get to help and I couldn't do it without them. They all donate their unwanted stuffed animals. They can also help at tagging and bagging events. I would also like other kids to set up *We Care Bears* chapters in their towns.

Do you see yourself as ordinary or extraordinary?

I'm just a regular kid. I'm a little special because I was adopted, so my parents picked me to be their kid - that's cool right?

What is the most important thing to you?

My family. I know what it's like to not have a family so I know that family is important.

What are your strengths?

I think I'm a good organizer and I am good at talking to people.

What are your weaknesses?

I'm still learning English and I have a hard time with spelling.

Does your project require you to focus on your strengths?

Yes, because I have to talk to a lot of people about my project and ask them to help me.

Who is your greatest role model and why?

I don't know - maybe my Mom and Dad because they teach me and love me and they always try to do nice things for people.

Of all the people in the world, who inspires you the most?

I don't know.

How/where/why did you learn to care globally?

My project isn't global it's just my project.

If you could change one thing in the world, what would it be?

I would like for no kids to be scared and alone.

What do you think are the ingredients for success?

Never give up. Maybe 10 people will say no but someone will say yes.

What is your global vision?

Just that everyone tries to do one nice thing a day.

What would be your message to the world?

My message is really for little kids and it is from my friend Paul Sikes' song. It is that you are never too small to do amazing things. If you see something that can make things better, do it. Tell someone, ask for help and do it.

If other kids wanted to start up their own magnificent project, what advice would you give them and what steps would you suggest they take?

First find a need in the community or world. Then find out who the helpers will be. Then DO IT. I have a favorite song by Paul Sikes and I make it my project's theme song. It is called 'The Seed' and it goes…

"Don't tell me you're too small to do amazing things… I was just a seed" and then it talks about all the things that just a seed (that turned into a tree) did.

http://wecarebears.webs.com

"May you always see the world through the eyes of a child."
~ C.J. Heck

Jordyn Schara

Hi, I'm Jordyn Schara. I am an Author, Teen Activist, Speaker and Founder/President of *HOPE (Helping Our Peers Excel)* a non-profit, and Founder/President of two community service projects: *C4C (Comics for Change)* and *WI P^2D^2 (Wisconsin Prescription Pill and Drug Disposal),* and Co-Founder/Vice-President of *Project READ (Reading Equipment for America's Defenders).* In addition, I have been recognized for my entrepreneurial initiatives with honors from the Volvo Adventure Award in Sweden and I was also selected to carry the torch in London for the 2012 Olympics.

My first service project was *Project READ*, started by my older brother Josh, and I helped him with it. It was a project that collected books, magazines and other reading material for the troops in Iraq. We then raised money to ship these materials overseas to areas where our local troops were stationed. I was in fifth grade when we started this project and I was immediately hooked on service. As soon as I saw the impact that our little project was having on people across the world who were sacrificing so much, I knew that I wanted to continue making an impact like that for the rest of my life.

Another community service project that I created inspires teens to get involved in their communities and it is called *C4C (Comics 4 Change)*. I am working with teens, parents, children, teachers and businesses to collect and purchase comics to distribute to under resourced youth to help them improve their reading skills.

The goal of *C4C* is to use the popular genre of comic books and graphic novels to motivate students to read. This is especially useful in hooking reluctant readers who have difficulty going from picture books to novels.

So far, I have held multiple comic book fairs where over 800 children have attended and *C4C* has given each child a free age-appropriate comic to help engage struggling, young readers to develop the skills necessary for reading more challenging works, including the classics.

C4C teen volunteers have also set up libraries at local homeless shelters, food pantries, clinics, hospitals, public libraries and police departments in two communities with over 500 comics. We are now looking to expand throughout the county.

Research proves that reading proficiently by the end of the third grade is a significant milestone and an indicator for later graduation. Third grade is a turning point at which children make the transition from learning to read to reading to learn. I want to inspire young people to develop a life-long love of reading in order to improve their literacy and academic skills.

My desire to create sustainable projects impacts our next generation who are just waiting for mentors to come along and help them get started. The projects that I start are able to be continued for years with new volunteers who can put their own creative touch to the project and in turn recruit others to help. This has a domino effect, where eventually I hope to touch thousands of lives either directly with my projects or indirectly by recruiting volunteers to engage in community service.

My mother always teases that I was never a child. I know that she is kidding, but there is always a dash of truth to these stories. She explained wistfully that I never believed in Santa and that she was never able to use reverse psychology on me, the way she was able to on my older brother.

Baby talk did not pass from my lips; my first words quickly became sentences and I would engage adults in conversation. Dolls did not fascinate me very much, but I loved to be read to. My brother was reading by then and wanting desperately to be at his level, I pretended to read books, making up the stories from the pictures on each page. Everyone was quite entertained by this, but I remember desperately wanting to read and believing that I would never learn.

These two characteristics of my childhood greatly influence who I am today. I read voraciously and I search for the truth in everything. If I discover an injustice, then it becomes my responsibility to make sure that the world is aware of it. Naturally, I have gravitated to journalism, where the pen wields mighty powers. I have been a reporter for our school newspaper for two years and was given a column this year. I also belong to Forensics and Mock Trial, where I am both the prosecutor and defending attorney. Last year I helped our team advance to state level for the first time in the school's history.

My immediate family isn't complete without my Grandma June. She and my Grandpa Lawrence helped to raise my brother and me while our parents worked. They were hard working farmers and didn't have material wealth, but made up for it with family, loyalty, love and faith. My favorite memories are when they still lived on the farm with the cats, dogs, cows, chickens, lambs and even a pet raccoon. Our family is very close and every holiday, the entire gang still gets together.

My Grandma's life is like a movie because she has gone through so many trials, and yet she has become stronger because of it. She married at 17, gave birth to seven children, and then came down with rheumatic fever. She was bed-ridden and had to re-learn how to walk. My Grandpa worked two jobs, so my Grandma had her hands full with managing a farm, a house and seven children. Grandma June wanted to be a nurse but never had the opportunity, so I promised her that I would graduate from college and pursue a career to honor her hard work.

I have a strong faith and firm morals based on how my grandparents helped to raise me. My Grandma grew up in an era of female submission, yet she is a very strong and intelligent woman. I respect her very much for overcoming obstacles and in honor of her, I plan on naming my future daughter Twila, my Grandma's real first name.

Through my commitment to my projects I have been blessed with many awards and honors including:

- Hometown Hero - Wisconsin State Assembly (2013)
- AXA Achiever - National Winner (2013)
- World Citizenship Award from Scouts of the World (2012)
- Coca-Cola National Scholar (2013)
- Featured as one of the top 10 stories of 2012 – Reedsburg Times Press (2012)
- World Citizenship Award from Scouts of the World (2012)
- GenerationOn Service Leaders Committee (2012-2013)
- Wisconsin Hero Award (2012)
- National Child Awareness Ambassador (2012)
- DoSomething.org – National Youth Advisory Council (2011-2012)
- DoSomething.org Club/Reedsburg – Founder/President (2011-2013)
- Leadership Wisconsin - Excellence Awards – Emerging Leader Award (2011)
- 2011 Leader of Tomorrow – National Winner (2011)
- United Nations Pilgrimage for Youth – Order of Oddfellows Delegate (2011)
- Nestle Very Best In Youth Award (NVBIY) - National Finalist (2011)
- Super Teen - National Winner (2011)
- Gloria Barron Prize for Young Heroes – National Runner Up (2010)
- Youth Serve America (YSA) National Youth Council (2010 - 2013)
- Get Ur Good On/Miley Cyrus Grant – International Winner (2010)

- Youth Service America's (YSA) - Everyday Young Hero (2010)
- The Prudential Spirit of Community Awards - State Winner (2009), National Winner (2012)
- VFW Outstanding Young Volunteer of the Year Award – State Winner (2009)
- American Red Cross Real Hero – Youth Good Samaritan Award (2009)
- President's Gold Volunteer Service Award (2008)

I have also been featured in many magazines and publications including Seventeen, Teen Vogue, Girls Life, Justine Magazine, Family Circle, Teen Life, Capricho (Brazil's Teen Magazine), Peace Jam, Do Something.org, Relate magazine, Youth Service America, GirlZone, Teens Now Talk, American Profile, CNN iReport, Earth911, Nickelodeon, among many others. I have just been selected by Teen Vogue magazine to fly to Arizona to attend CGIU (Clinton Global Initiative University) where I will get to meet Chelsea Clinton and her parents. I am very excited!

My Top 10 List

10. Expand my drug collection program, ***WI P^2D^2***
9. Expand my **Comics 4 Change** (C4C) program
8. Publish the book I am working on
7. Be a war correspondent
6. Own my own home
5. Work for an accredited publication
4. Never be afraid to be myself
3. Never lose my sense of humor
2. Travel not as a tourist but as a citizen of the world
1. Be pleased with the legacy I have left in the world

My top 10 list is a list of things that I want to achieve and of course it morphs a little each day as I too change with each of my experiences. My principle belief of "Never Be Afraid to Be Myself" came to me when I was in elementary school. It was there that I started to see how some children were judged and criticized because of where they lived or the clothes they wore (or couldn't afford to

Magnificent Kids!

wear). The bullying only intensified in middle school and I decided that I would not be a willow and bend because of these bullies.

My clothes are mostly second hand and I live outside of town, so I'm not one of the popular girls, but you wouldn't know it by looking at me. I walk with my head held high and I stand up for myself and others. I choose my role models carefully; accepting myself for who I am because it is what makes me JORDYN. You may think being involved in a dozen extra-curriculars, working part-time, creating my own non-profit and then starting three successful community service projects is hard work, but nothing compares with having to negotiate your way around bullies every day and they are not just students - they can be teachers and administrators.

I feel that I am a stronger and more confident person because of these trials and I haven't become a 'cookie-cutter' teen. I have learned that I need to always stand up for what I believe in and question what other people tell me. That doesn't mean doubt what others say - but actually think about what they say and carefully consider it before just believing it. I realize that these experiences have given me the courage to lead not follow, to make the right choices - not just the easiest ones, to fearlessly pursue my biggest dreams and to be confident when I am going against the grain.

I want others to know that a positive self-image assures them of power, strength, ability and confidence, which is why I spend so much of my time mentoring young teens with my community service projects. My goal is to not only give kids and teens the opportunities to see firsthand the issues in their communities and around the globe, but to also give them the tools they need to respond and become a part of the solution.

Jordyn Schara

What does the word 'magnificent' mean to you?

Magnificent means going above and beyond what is expected.

What do you give to the world?

I give inspiration to others by demonstrating that you can make a difference.

Why is this important to you?

Because I feel that it is everyone's duty to help others and when one person becomes empowered it helps the next person. It becomes a chain reaction.

Why did you choose the project/idea that you did?

For this question I will refer to my drug collection project. After reading about the death of teens in the state from prescription drug abuse, I created ***WI P^2D^2***, which stands for Wisconsin Prescription Pill and Drug Disposal. Our medicine cabinets are now the new drug dealers. The prescription drug medicines that we leave unsecured in our medicine cabinets are fuelling the newest drug problem among America's teens – Prescription Drug Abuse.

My goal with ***WI P^2D^2*** is to educate the public about prescription drug abuse, how to properly dispose of their unwanted drugs and how to safely store the drugs they choose to keep in their homes. So far, I have held multiple drug collection events, created 10 permanent drug collection programs, hosted a flu shot clinic, a free sharps disposal, a free mercury thermometer swap and have helped keep over 1,000,000 pounds of drugs out of the hands of young children and teens.

I have also purchased several 24/7 drug drop off boxes for communities, engaged high school students to paint and decorate the containers, helped cities purchase incinerators to save on disposal

Magnificent Kids!

costs, been the first teen in Wisconsin to win a municipal state grant for drug collection/disposal, mentored teens and adults across the country with their programs and I have become a national spokesperson for teen activism. I have partnered with another drug collection program and P^2D^2 has now spread across the country into more than 22 states.

How old were you when you began your project?

I was 12 when I started out by helping my brother with ***Project READ*** (Reading Equipment for America's Defenders) and 14 when I started my non-profit ***HOPE*** (Helping Our Peers Excel) and ***WI P^2D^2*** (Prescription Pill and Drug Disposal).

How did you go about getting it started?

A concoction of drugs - including antibiotics, anti-convulsants, acne medication, mood stabilizers and sex hormones - have been found in the drinking water supplies of at least 41 million Americans, according to an Associated Press investigation. The federal government doesn't require any testing and hasn't set safety limits for drugs in water. Even users of bottled water and home filtration systems are exposed. Some bottlers simply repackage tap water and do not typically treat or test for pharmaceuticals. The same goes for the makers of home filtration systems.

Contamination is not confined to the United States. More than 100 different drugs have been detected in waterways throughout the world. Fish and prawns in China that were exposed to treated wastewater had shortened life spans. In Norway, Atlantic salmon that were exposed to estrogen in the North Sea had severe reproductive problems. Recent studies have found alarming effects on human cells and wildlife. Male fish are being feminized and female fish have developed male genital organs. Recent research has found that small amounts of medication exposure have caused human breast cancer cells to grow faster, kidney cells to grow too slowly and blood cells to show signs of inflammation. Scientists are researching the extent of this contamination, but our government is hurting us by not proactively addressing the problem.

I decided to meet this challenge head on, to spread awareness and provide communities with a safe way to dispose of these toxic drugs by creating *WI P^2D^2* (Wisconsin Prescription Pill and Drug Disposal), which is a teen organized drug collection program that is dedicated to keeping the water systems of the world safe from the irreversible damage that is caused by the improper disposal of medication. I have accomplished this by spreading awareness and providing countless communities with permanent disposal containers and incinerators, as well as through the use of mentorship for both adult and youth leaders.

Since then, I discovered an even more urgent reason to create *WI P^2D^2*. The prescription drugs and Over-The-Counter (OTC) medicines that we leave unsecured in our medicine cabinets are fuelling the newest drug problem among America's teens – Prescription and OTC Drug Abuse. More people abuse prescription drugs than cocaine, heroin and methamphetamine combined. Teens are taking prescription and OTC drugs from their parents' and friends' medicine cabinets and abusing them. In the newspapers we regularly see police reports of home break-ins that report prescription drugs as one of the items stolen or obituaries of teens who have died of a prescription drug overdose.

When I started my program, people were disposing of their medicines by pouring them down the drain, flushing them down the toilet or throwing them out in the trash because this is what they were told to do and they weren't provided any alternatives. All of these methods are seriously detrimental to our environment. The Environmental Protection Agency (EPA) states that the sewage treatment systems are not specifically engineered to remove pharmaceuticals. My goals were twofold:

A) to educate the world that improper disposal of drugs contaminates our ground water, which results in deformities in amphibians and unknown genetic problems for humans; and

Magnificent Kids!

B) to provide communities with a safe means of disposing of their drugs. Since our state and federal governments were not even acknowledging that this danger existed let alone trying to address it by providing us with secure disposal options, the impact was significant.

To start my drug program, I contacted the DEA (Drug Enforcement Agency), the DNR (Department of Natural Resources) the EPA and the Department of Justice but none of these governmental agencies were willing to tackle this serious problem or help me with my project. I decided that I would make a difference by conducting a drug collection in my hometown on my own. This was a monumental task as it is illegal to collect or accept prescription drugs from someone and the cost to dispose of these drugs is prohibitive.

Once I worked out the details of my program, I contacted my local police chief and made a presentation to the city council. They gave me a standing ovation and even provided me with funds to start my program. At that point, I made presentations to the local hospital, pharmacists, civic organizations, business leaders and schools to recruit volunteers and spread awareness. I launched a marketing campaign by creating my own brochures and flyers and distributed them around town. I recruited volunteers and made posters, had banners designed and created funny and engaging t-shirts. The most unique and interesting way that we promoted *WI P^2D^2* was when we created a mascot costume named, "Phil the Pill Bottle". Predictably, Phil is a huge hit!

I became the first teen organization to have written and been awarded a Wisconsin State drug grant. This money helped support *WI P^2D^2*. When I discovered that a state grant was available to help communities start a drug collection program, I asked my town's grant writer if he would apply and he said NO. I then asked a neighboring community if they would apply for the grant. They said that they would apply for the grant, but that they would keep the money and not share it with my hometown. I then decided, at the age of 14, to apply for the grant myself. Imagine my surprise when I discovered that I won the grant and the neighboring town's grant was disqualified. I then contacted both towns and informed them that I won and that I was splitting the grant between them. At that point they became my greatest supporters.

So far we have held multiple drug collection events, started programs in 10 communities in Wisconsin, hosted a free sharps disposal and a free mercury thermometer swap and have helped keep over 1,000,000 pounds of drugs out of our groundwater. ***WI P^{2}D^2*** has helped purchase several 24/7 drug drop off boxes for communities, engaged high school students to paint and decorate the containers, helped cities purchase incinerators to save on disposal costs, mentored teens and adults across the country with their programs, raised over $90,000 and it has become a national model for teen-created drug collection programs. Furthermore, ***WI P^{2}D^2*** is the largest teen-run, self-sustainable, drug collection program in the world!

WI P^{2}D^2 has joined forces with a dynamic science teacher/mentor from Illinois who had his own drug collection program and now P^{2}D^2 has spread across the country into over 22 states. My specific goal with ***WI P^{2}D^2*** is to educate the public about prescription and OTC drug abuse, provide a means of properly disposing of their unwanted drugs and instruct the public about how to safely store the drugs they choose to keep in their homes. Spreading awareness by working with local youth, volunteers, law enforcement, local, state and national government, teachers, businesses and civic organizations is the only way to save our teens from prescription drug abuse. Spreading the word about prescription drug abuse across the country is my next step. I am doing this by making presentations and speeches at conferences (Safer Use Prevents Abuse Coalition, Family Ties/Children Come First Conference, WEA Trust), recording a Public Safety Announcement warning parents about this epidemic among teens, speaking to the media and lawmakers. I am currently working with my Wisconsin lawmakers to enact a bill to help every community in Wisconsin to have its own program – cost free.

I am on a mission to mobilize the energy, ingenuity and compassion of young people to discover their power and potential to solve real

Magnificent Kids!

world problems through service and service learning. My goal is to not only give kids and teens the opportunities to see, firsthand, the issues in the communities and around the globe, but also to give them the tools that they need to respond and become a part of the solution.

Who is your project benefiting, and how?

My audience is: young children who risk dying from taking drugs that they think are candy; teens who 'take' these drugs from friends' and families' homes; elderly people who are overmedicated and store the drugs that they don't use or need; anyone who drinks water.

Who were the key people that supported you, and how?

First of all my parents, teachers, community leaders, mentor/teacher Paul Ritter, Steve Lyons, and national organizations such as: YSA, DoSomething.org, Coca-Cola, Volvo International, Adventure Award, Prudential Spirit of Community Award, Finding Fearless, and Case Foundation.

How much financial assistance did you have, and from whom?

In the very beginning, I went to all of my local civic organizations looking for donations and I received several hundred dollars. Then I started applying to local and state grants and received several thousand dollars. Eventually, I applied for national grants and received several thousands of dollars.

How will you keep your project going into the future?

There are dozens and dozens of national grant programs that I will turn to for funding for my future programs.

How have your peers responded to you setting up the project, and do they (or can they) get involved in any way?

I provide them with opportunities to get involved by either volunteering on my projects or by starting their own projects. I am always recruiting teen volunteers for my projects and my non-profit *HOPE* strives to help others start their own projects. Many students congratulated me on my projects and asked to help. I have actually helped four students start their own projects and one of them has won an award.

Do you see yourself as ordinary or extraordinary?

I see myself as an ordinary person who is trying to do extraordinary things.

What is the most important thing to you?

Never wasting a day of my life.

What are your strengths?

Public speaking and never taking no for an answer.

What are your weaknesses?

Waking up in the morning.

Does your project require you to focus on your strengths?

Yes, I am constantly asked to give interviews and presentations. Also, I was forced to jump many hurdles that were placed in my way.

Magnificent Kids!

Who is your greatest role model and why?

Taylor Swift because she worked very hard to get to where she is. She fought against ageism and when she became famous, she never forgot her fans. I was blessed to be able to meet her last summer when my friends and I were chosen from an audience of 15,000 fans to go back stage to the Red Room to meet her!

Of all the people in the world, who inspires you the most?

Lisa Ling

How/where/why did you learn to care globally?

Probably with my parents as they instilled in me, at a young age, to think about what I can do to make a difference.

If you could change one thing in the world, what would it be?

I would want to open people's eyes to the idea that they <u>can</u> make a difference.

What do you think are the ingredients for success?

Creativity, entrepreneurship, drive and tenacity

What is your global vision?

A world where everyone helps everyone else out

What would be your message to the world?

Don't be so content with your own life that you don't notice the struggles in other people's lives.

If other kids wanted to start up their own magnificent project, what advice would you give them and what steps would you suggest they take?

I would suggest that kids connect with a mentor (teacher, civic leader, parent, etc.), then research other projects to come up with an idea, then research the issue once a project has been chosen, and then connect and network with community and civic leaders. They will help you raise money, spread the word, reach volunteers, etc.

www.helpingourpeersexcel.com

"Listen earnestly to anything your children want to tell you, no matter what. If you don't listen eagerly to the little stuff when they are little, they won't tell you the big stuff when they are big, because to them all of it has always been big stuff."
~ Catherine M. Wallace

Liva Adelstorp

Hi my name is Liva. I was born in Denmark but I have lived in Bali my whole life. When I was little, my family and I would go to the ocean often. I loved the beach and I did all the usual kid things like running in the water and building sand castles. But I was scared to swim in the ocean because of all the dirt and rubbish. When I grew older, I loved swimming in the ocean, watching the fish and corals and floating in the salty water. I am so lucky to have grown up in Bali with some of the most amazing coral reefs and underwater life. But I was still very frustrated about the pollution.

By the time I turned nine, I had seen some documentaries and pictures of animals caught in plastic bags and old fishing nets and I realized how bad trash is for the ocean. I worried about the animals becoming extinct and I wished I could do something about it. I wanted to see all my favorite animals like dolphins, turtles, whales, jelly fish, sharks and sting rays living freely in a clean ocean. Every time we went to the beach, I thought and thought about what I could do to help make the ocean a better place.

Magnificent Kids!

Then one day when I was ten, I went snorkelling with a group of friends and we took our cameras. Again there was a lot of trash stuck to corals and floating on the surface. I told my Mom I wanted to do something about the rubbish and we started thinking about things that might help solve the problem.

Suddenly I thought, "What if all of us collected the rubbish while snorkeling?" and the idea came to me to make an ***underwater rubbish collection bag*** that we could strap to a belt around our waists. The luckiest thing about it was that the Green School in Bali had just opened a competition that was called, "The Greenest Student on Earth" which was a great motivator to start my idea and produce my first prototype. I entered the competition with my ***underwater rubbish collection bag***.

We started thinking about how the bag would look and how we would get people to use them. At first it seemed just too big and we weren't sure how to make it grow. We thought the "Greenest Student on Earth" competition would help to raise awareness. There were times when I wanted to give up but Mom kept inspiring me. We approached a dive centre in Sanur and they made the first prototype bags for us. From that we received our first order for the dive school. Currently 'Phoenix Garment Factory' produces my bags and I have had a lot of interest from people wanting to buy them.

I recently went on my very first dive and we took six of my bags and collected rubbish in them. It was fantastic to see how the bags worked first hand. The bags also come with gloves and scissors so we were able to try them out as well. 'Project Aware' will be receiving the profits from any sales of the bags, and this will help them to keep raising public awareness about the problems our oceans and animals are facing.

There's only one Earth and all the animals we share the planet with are living beings so I really think we should respect them and be nice to them and clean up all the rubbish. When I'm older I want to be an ocean environmentalist so that I can help a lot more.

Liva Adelstorp

What does the word 'magnificent' mean to you?

Big, beautiful, amazing, extraordinary

What do you give to the world?

I help to clean the ocean and I try to spread public awareness of pollution and how we can all help the Earth.

Why is this important to you?

Because I care a lot about the Earth and I care about the animals. I would like to see a beautiful coral reef whenever I dive.

Why did you choose the project/idea that you did?

I chose it because I love the ocean and I really wanted to do something for it.

How old were you when you began your project?

10 years old

How did you go about getting it started?

Many people encouraged me. My Mom helped me find materials and Minni (Crystal divers) gave me ideas about how to collect trash. Janma (Phoenix Garment Factory) helped with the prototype.

Who is your project benefiting, and how?

Project Aware, the ocean and ocean animals. I give all the profit to Project Aware. It helps the ocean because it will take out a lot of the debris and it will help the ocean animals because they won't get stuck in nets or plastic. It will also help birds because when they dive for fish, they sometimes retrieve plastic, not fish. Project Aware also helps people so they can enjoy the ocean. If the oceans are not healthy, humans will get sick or maybe even not survive.

Who were the key people that supported you, and how?

My Mom, Minni the owner of crystal divers, and Janma the owner of Phoenix Garment factory. My Mom, because she always believed I could do it. Minni, because she supported me, bought my bags and taught me how to dive.

How much financial assistance did you have, and from whom?

Maybe around $300 from my Mom and people who gave me donations. Mini at Crystal Divers offered me a $100 discount at Junior Divers if I started up a blog about my bags. Of course I took up her offer.

How will you keep your project going into the future?

I want to sell to dive schools and I would like to ask PADI (Professional Association of Diving Instructors) if they can help me spread the word.

How have your peers responded to you setting up the project, and do they (or can they) get involved in any way?

They think it's really cool. They can donate and buy bags. They can help spread the word.

Do you see yourself as ordinary or extraordinary?

Extraordinary.

What is the most important thing to you?

Mother Nature, saving the ocean and the planet.

What are your strengths?

My love for nature and the ocean, when I want something I don't give up and I'm not afraid to try new things.

What are your weaknesses?

I'm not sure.

Does your project require you to focus on your strengths?

Yes.

Who is your greatest role model and why?

My mom is my greatest role model as she helps me through everything and she also cares a lot about animals. She always reminds me to clean up the rubbish I find and she has a big connection to nature.

Of all the people in the world, who inspires you the most?

I am very inspired by the people in Project Aware and all the people who work to save the ocean. I met a really nice lady from Greenpeace and she gave me a flag and talked to me about all the things they did. She said she really liked my idea and she really inspired me.

How/where/why did you learn to care globally?

I just do... When I was home schooling, I started searching out organizations and saw what they were doing for the world. These things really inspired me. I saw how the planet is in really bad shape right now and we need to do much better with the way we treat the animals and the planet.

If you could change one thing in the world, what would it be?

Clean up all the pollution.

What do you think are the ingredients for success?

Don't let anything get in the way.

What is your global vision?

For the world to have billions of rain forests, no trash and less plastic produced. Also, for people to live in peace with the animals. I imagine trees everywhere and barely any cars or motorbikes causing pollution. No trash by the roadside or in the oceans or the forests.

What would be your message to the world?

Don't be cruel to the animals, plant trees instead of cutting them down, clean up the ocean instead of throwing more trash into it and stop creating so much trash from the big factories because there's only one planet. You need to think about your great grand kids and think about how the world will look when they are here.

If other kids wanted to start up their own magnificent project, what advice would you give them and what steps would you suggest they take?

Take the leap. Don't let anything get in the way. Have fun doing it.

livasgreensea.weebly.com

"The small hopes and plans and pleasures
of children should be tenderly respected
by grown-up people, and
never rudely thwarted or ridiculed."
~ Louisa May Alcott, Little Men

Louis Robinson

Hi, my name is Louis Robinson. I'm 14 years old and I love to surf, well body board actually. I'm also the creator of **Beco Bags** which are body board bags made from recycled material. Here's how it started...

I'm originally from Adelaide in Australia and my weekends were never complete without skateboarding with my mates. My family and I went to Bali a couple of times for a holiday and I went body boarding with my own instructor. When I was 13, my family surprised me by asking if I would like to live in Bali. My first reaction was, "No, I don't want to move." In Australia, all my friends and I were having heaps of fun and I couldn't really imagine how I could have a good life without all the good things I had at home. I think I reacted this way because I didn't want to move out of my comfort zone. My parents talked to me about a school they had found in Bali called the Green School. Academics have never really been my strong point and they thought the Green School would be more suited to my learning style. I did my own research into the school and initially I really wasn't convinced it was the place for me. I thought it seemed like a school full of hippies. My passion for body boarding grew over the months following and I started to think, "Why shouldn't I want to live in Bali? It's got some of the best surfing in the world. Well maybe it won't be so bad."

We went back to Bali and my parents organised for me to have a tour of the Green School where I met some really cool people and it resonated with me straight away. I went to a private school in Australia and for the kind of person I am, it really didn't fit. At the Green School they focus more on how and what you do rather than how you look. I understand that there are certain standards regarding appearance, but I have long hair. I don't think having long hair should be a reason for you to stay in on the weekend!

It took a while for me to get in as I have dyslexia, so a school like that can't really take on too many kids with learning barriers as it's harder to get resources to assist. But when I finally did get in, it was an awesome moment. It was like, "I'm moving to Bali now. OMG it's really happening." I had 6 months to go and then I would be in Indonesia. To be honest, I was counting down the days until I was out of my old school. My parents had already bought land in Bali with the sole purpose of giving me the opportunity to go to the Green School. Not many kids get the opportunity to learn this way so I felt very privileged. Heaps of kids learn through mainstream and for some people it's the right way with the strict rules etc, but for me it's not what I need. They interviewed me and they knew how deep my love for animals was, so they determined that the Green School was the place for me. It suits my personality a lot.

Once I was at the school I learnt that we do a Quest project where you work on something for 6 months and then you do a presentation at the end. I had just bought a new body board and needed to get a new bag for it. After driving around Bali and thinking about it for a while, it came to me. When elections are held in Bali, they go a little crazy with elections banners. These banners end up in the already overcrowded waste system and often in the rivers. I realised these banners would be terrific to recycle into body board bags. I decided to use the banners once I saw the fabric up close as I knew it would be water proof and thought that it was perfect to make a great bag because Bali does tend to have an overabundance of banners at election times. This way I also help the environment.

I found out about a company that employs people with disabilities who make things, so I thought if I get the banners, I could ask them to make the bags. I got in touch with them. I don't know if this is politically correct or not, but I started worrying about whether I was being disrespectful and I thought I might be pushing them because they have a physical and /or intellectual disability. Then I felt bad about asking them.

I had further thoughts about the bag and just knew I had the right idea so I started to really focus on it. The Green School started putting our project introduction videos up on the website and within a couple of days, I had people coming up to me saying they would like to help me. Then a few days later I was at Echo Beach lying down enjoying the sun and someone came up to me and said,
"Hey, are you Louis?"
I thought I was in trouble but then he asked,
"Are you the board bag guy?"
I wondered how he knew that. Then I remembered Youtube. He said, "Do you want to come and talk to us? We own a factory and we produce clothing for Bali Boat Shed".

So I talked to them and they offered to design and make the first bags free of charge. I was left thinking that this was an opportunity people only dream about. At the moment, I'm still working with them. I'm getting them to make my last two bags that I will pay for and I'm sending them off to the world famous body boarder Mike Stewart, 9 times world champion.

I sent off some emails to world famous body boarders and body board magazines thinking that they might not get back to me but there's nothing to lose. Two months later I was at school doing a science project and checking my phone when I shouldn't have been, and there it was; an email from Mike Stewart! I lost control. Then I had to do a double take. Really? Wow! Is this a dream? This is Mike Stewart. People can only dream of this. So I ended up Skyping with him a couple of times and it all got a bit too exciting and I really was

Magnificent Kids!

on a high. Mike was very interested in my bag and I dream of collaborating with him in the future. Dad owns a business and he has always told me that it's best to grow things steadily. If you rise too quickly you will also drop very quickly, and that's what happened. I got super excited and then the holidays came so I went surfing. I am someone who needs motivation to keep me energized and I'm the kind of person who loses interest a bit if I lose momentum. Being away from school and the motivation of the people at the school, created a big drop.

Anyway, the good news is, I'm back into it and hoping for a known brand to allow me to piggyback **Beco Boards** with their line to create better sales. I would really like to get them into stores in Hawaii, and in particular develop a partnership with Mike Stewart's 'Science Body Boards'. In the future I am also hoping to design a body board sock made out of bamboo. But for now, I just need someone to take a chance on a 14 year old kid. I volunteered at the Bali Street Children project with my Mum a few times and it really meant a lot to me. A percentage of the bag sales will be going to the project so the kids there can have an improved life.

What does the word 'magnificent' mean to you?

The word magnificent to me is a word that strongly describes a person, place, or thing's beauty.

Louis Robinson

What do you give to the world?

I hope that I give energy to the world. I see myself as a fairly energetic person and I think it is crucial to try and do all things with as much energy as possible. I also I hope I can bring new ideas to the world.

Why is this important to you?

Bringing energy to the world is important because it lets people make boring things fun for example, maths. If you made maths into an energy and fun filled activity I am sure you would capture the minds of many children.

Why did you choose the project/idea that you did?

I didn't really choose this project it just came to me, but I decided to go with it because of people around me encouraging me and telling me on how this idea actually had the capacity to become something.

How old were you when you began your project?

14 years old.

How did you go about getting it started?

At the moment, I am still getting it started, and sometimes I have had to remind myself to keep up that energy!

Who is your project benefiting, and how?

Hopefully my project benefits people indirectly but I am giving a portion of the profits to the Bali Street Children organization.

Who were the key people that supported you, and how?

I would say that everyone has been a huge help. But to be particular, my whole family, my school, Mike Stewart and the Bali Boat Shed team.

How much financial assistance did you have, and from whom?

So far none but I will need some to take this where I want it.

How will you keep your project going into the future?

I plan to keep the energy in the business but I also want to keep looking at new ideas to keep myself inspired and constantly thinking.

How have your peers responded to you setting up the project, and do they (or can they) get involved in any way?

Everyone has been really supportive. My brother is helping me with the design of the project as he is a graphic designer but I am trying to keep this as my own, more than anything.

Do you see yourself as ordinary or extraordinary?

I would say that I am an ordinary person with lots of passion and energy.

What is the most important thing to you?

Energy. I love having energy, it makes everything better, for example you cannot have fun when you have no energy.

What are your strengths?

My energy
My enthusiasm
Strong minded

What are your weaknesses?

Lazy
Find it hard to focus
Doing the mathematical side of things

Does your project require you to focus on your strengths?

Yeah, my project does require me to focus on my strengths. I think if I constantly focused on my weaknesses it would limit me from taking this to the highest point.

Who is your greatest role model and why?

I would say at the moment, it's Mike Stewart, a nine times world champion body boarder. He would be my greatest role model because of what he has done and how he still is the most humble and kind person.

Of all the people in the world, who inspires you the most?

Oh god, I have no idea. The Balinese people are really inspiring with their ability to be so happy when some of them have so little.

How/where/why did you learn to care globally?

I think I always knew about it but at my school I learnt how to put it forward and take action. I learnt it because I am surrounded by it at my school.

Magnificent Kids!

If you could change one thing in the world, what would it be?

The part of the human brain which says we need to dominate. This would stop the destroying of forests and the inhumane ways we keep animals. It would also mean there would not be leaders who want to control millions of people and put their lives in jeopardy.

What do you think are the ingredients for success?

I think that there are four things you must have:
Energy
Listening
Patience
Being able to make decisions that not everyone will like

What is your global vision?

To bring justice where there is injustice.

What would be your message to the world?

Have fun whenever you can, think big and you will go big.

If other kids wanted to start up their own magnificent project, what advice would you give them and what steps would you suggest they take?

I think the best thing to do is just do it. If you really believe that one of your ideas has the capability of becoming something, go for it. I have found that when you are young, people tend to listen more. Do not make promises when everything is good, sometimes you cannot live up to those promises. And last of all, keep the energy and keep reminding yourself of the goal.

Luca Berardi

My name is Luca, I am 10 years old and I live in Kenya. I was born in Italy, lived in Thailand for two years, then moved to Romania for a year and back to Thailand for three years, before relocating to Kenya. I sing, play the piano and act. During my free time I write books and I am a great lover of nature and wildlife. I am currently a music student at Wynton House of Music, where I learn piano and voice. I would like to become an actor and a singer one day. I have been singing in public performances since I was 4 and I'm now pursuing my dreams with my piano and voice lessons. I have passed the Grade 3 musical theatre exams with a distinction at the London College of Music and I have recently completed Grade 2 piano as well. I have participated in various school drama and musical productions in Kenya and abroad. In 2013, I released my first single "A Better Place" with Grandpa Records, Kenya. You can find the video clip to this on YouTube if you search *Luca: A Better Place*. Of course, I am also a keen fan of cartoons and other TV programmes and I love to go to the cinema whenever possible.

Apart from music, my main interests are writing books (little books for children which I hope to publish one day) and animal-related topics. I read a lot about nature and I'm currently writing a program aimed at saving endangered animals, which I hope will reach a lot of people. According to the *International Union for Conservation of Nature (2010)*, over 17 thousand animal species are endangered. They are classified as vulnerable, endangered or critically endangered. That's a mind-blowing number and although the amount is still small when compared to the number of species officially described, you can still imagine the huge loss of biodiversity that each of these species takes with it when it becomes extinct. Playing with stuffed toys as a small child I was always interested in animals, but it was later, through books, TV programmes and the internet, that I realised how severely the problem of shrinking biodiversity negatively affects our planet and its long-term survival.

As a result, I started thinking of what a tiny boy like me, and thousands of others like me, could do to try and prevent this tragedy. I came up with a dream; a dream and a project. The project is called **Y.A.R.H *(Young Animal Rescue Heroes)*** and young people like you and me can be the real heroes of our time if we are able to protect the species that are currently endangered. Awareness is one of our main tools. Without awareness, actions that could be undertaken at a very low cost and with great effect may not even be taken into consideration because they are simply not thought of. Awareness is also a powerful weapon that does not necessarily need millions of shillings. Awareness is each of us sharing the things we learn about with our families and friends and by doing so, the message will be repeated through new channels every day.

Y.A.R.H invites children from all over the world to be part of this initiative and work together to save our endangered animals starting in Kenya and eventually reaching every region of the world. ***Y.A.R.H*** aims to network with other children to create awareness within society of the issues endangered animals face. Activities include public speeches, animal-themed drawing and writing competitions, celebrating animals through children's fun days and music and educating communities about the importance of conservation. ***Y.A.R.H*** also works with communities to help build creativity based micro-economies as sources of income, to train animal rescuers and to raise awareness about ways to reduce threats that lead to the endangering of habitats.

I also partnered with Chandaria Industries which is a well known leader in recycling. Recycling relieves pressure on deforestation. The recycling project encourages families, offices and schools to donate their waste paper to Chandria and *Y.A.R.H* receives the funds to help with animal conservation.

I feel great that we are doing something about the environment but at the same time I feel sad for the animals that are endangered because of the current environmental degradation. I will continue my work to identify possible ways through which *Y.A.R.H* can become an effective force and I'll be delighted to share any progress and development with those of you who would like to stay in touch. But in the meantime, please think of yourselves as mighty players in a game that we do not want to end with our planet losing out, and do whatever you can to spread the message that saving endangered animals is, in the end, saving ourselves.

What does the word 'magnificent' mean to you?

It means being an extraordinary child who wants to make the world a better place.

What do you give to the world?

I give peace, love and happiness.

Why is this important to you?

Because if there is no peace there will be endless war, if there is no love then everybody will hate each other, and if there is no happiness then I don't know what kind of world this is.

Why did you choose the project/idea that you did?

Because I wanted to create awareness to save our endangered species.

How old were you when you began your project?

I was 8 years old.

How did you go about getting it started?

I first thought about the name which is ***Y.A.R.H (Young Animal Rescue Heroes)*** and then I got support from Chandaria Industries which is a paper recycling company.

Who is your project benefiting, and how?

The animals, because when you spread the word and create awareness, saving the animals might just be a little bit easier.

Who were the key people that supported you, and how?

Chandaria Industries for recycling paper.

How much financial assistance did you have, and from whom?

More than $2,000 from my savings and support from Chandaria.

How will you keep your project going into the future?

By continuing to create awareness and hopefully we will get more support.

How have your peers responded to you setting up the project, and do they (or can they) get involved in any way?

When I first thought of the *Y.A.R.H* I wanted to go global right away because I thought there was no time to lose. My Mom tried to convince me to start locally and then go global. After a long time of arguing, I agreed. So children from all over the world can join the *Y.A.R.H* by simply saying yes and saying the *Y.A.R.H* pledge: "I _____ promise to save and love wildlife and nature and respect them."

Do you see yourself as ordinary or extraordinary?

I see myself as an ordinary person who is trying to make a difference.

What is the most important thing to you?

For everyone, every animal and every country to live in harmony.

What are your strengths?

Music and animals

What are your weaknesses?

I cannot stand news of animals being killed.

Does your project require you to focus on your strengths?

Yes, that strength gives me passion, strength and love for them.

Who is your greatest role model and why?

Crocodile hunter Steve Irwin, because I was inspired by him to do this project.

Of all the people in the world, who inspires you the most?

Barack Hussein Obama because he showed the world that everything is possible when he said, "Yes we can!"

How/where/why did you learn to care globally?

From the internet, documentaries, books and most of all my family.

If you could change one thing in the world, what would it be?

I would change people's greed for money and let them be a little bit more sensible.

What do you think are the ingredients for success?

Hard work, passion and not ever giving up.

What is your global vision?

A world with peace, love for all animals and that animals are not harmed by us. I want to see everyone living in harmony.

What would be your message to the world?

Never to give up and make the change that we all want, to really come true.

If other kids wanted to start up their own magnificent project, what advice would you give them and what steps would you suggest they take?

Follow their dream project, let the passion lead them and not to look back.

Steps: Think of how it could work, discuss it with those close to them and find professional help about getting started because in some cases you will need to register with authorities, and then bring other stakeholders on board.

http://yarhkenya.blogspot.com
yarhkenya@gmail.com

Magnificent Kids!

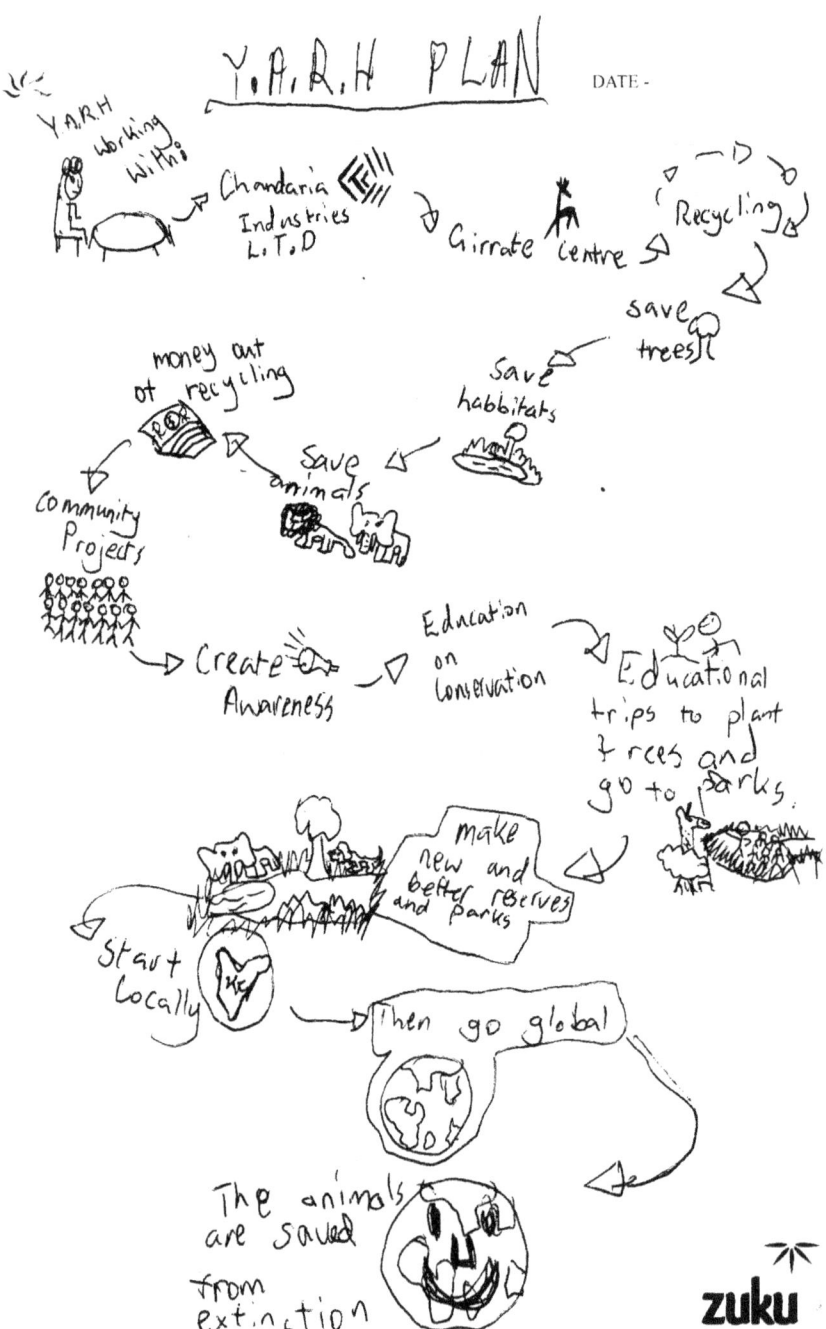

Max Wallack

When I was very young I was invited to participate in a Davidson Young Scholar conference at Lake Tahoe. There were about 20 Davidson Young Scholars and their families at the event. We stayed in a hotel up in Tahoe. I remember the sign as we entered the hotel building, "Don't leave the doors open. Bears will enter." That was pretty shocking to a five year old from Boston. I also remember the wonderful feeling of piloting Bob Davidson's boat on Lake Tahoe as he stood behind me. I tend to overheat very easily, and I even remember how the counselors took care of me after I vomited all over the activity tent. But, mostly I remember the words that Jan Davidson told me. She said she believed that anyone who had the ability to help another person had the responsibility to help them. I left Lake Tahoe believing that it was my responsibility to help others.

My first opportunity came when I was six. We had just purchased our first minivan, only to find that my great grandmother who lived with my family couldn't get into it. The step up was too high. We tried conventional step stools, but this left her feeling too dependent because we had to place the footstool and then pick it up after she got in. I thought it might be a good idea to make a step stool with a handle attached. That way she could hold onto the handle for balance and then use the handle to pull the step stool up into the minivan with her.

So began my first invention, the 'Great Granny Booster Step'. I never set out to invent something. I only noticed a need and tried to figure out how to remedy the situation. Soon after, I learned that NSTA Craftsman was holding an invention competition about inventing new tools. I entered the 'Great Granny Booster Step', and it won first place. We were invited to Chicago and the whole family headed out, this time in the minivan. I had many amazing experiences in Chicago. It gave me the opportunity to meet other kid inventors. Then, Great Grams, as I called her, was interviewed about how she felt about my building the step for her.

Something else important happened on that trip to Chicago. At one point, my family got lost on Lower Wacker Drive. It seems there is a whole system of roads that runs right under downtown Chicago's Million Dollar Mile. So, right under where the wealthiest people are shopping, there is a completely different world. That's where I first saw many homeless people, mostly sleeping in garbage bags. We spent a long time under there, driving in circles, actually ending up in the underground police car impound lot. I know that by the time we emerged from that underground world, my perspectives on many things had changed. I was particularly struck with the irony of these people living right below the wealthiest shopping district. There were two parallel worlds, co-existing: one on street level and one 30 feet below street level. I recall, at the invention awards ceremony, telling Bob Villa that I knew it was my responsibility to invent something to help those homeless people.

What doesn't work for me is to sit down and think, "What can I invent to help those people?" Many people have asked me what it takes to be a kid inventor. I've thought about that and decided that what it takes is being very observant. A person has to notice what is happening around him, and notice what people really need. You need to tuck that information into the back of your mind and keep it there until you see the solution that could make a difference in someone's life. In Chicago, I filed away the needs I saw among those homeless people. A few years later, I noticed an invention contest sponsored by Intel and ByKidsForKids. It was a challenge to use recycled materials to help people. Suddenly, I remembered those people underground in Chicago. I decided to think of a way to use recycled materials to help the homeless. Knowing that Styrofoam is almost impossible to break down or recycle and that it is a great insulating material, I decided to try to construct a shelter using Styrofoam peanuts from packing materials. The result was the 'Home Dome' and it won first place nationally. Several months later, some senators invited me to Washington D.C. to display the 'Home Dome' in the Russell Senate Office Building. There were also victims of Hurricane Katrina there who said that the 'Home Dome' was superior to some of the shelters that they had to live in.

I was still very young when I first decided to pursue a career in medicine. My early experiences helped me grasp the importance of what I might accomplish if I could succeed at practicing medicine with compassion. I can still recall, at the age of nine, with sleepy eyes, taking my post for the night. It was my turn to sleep on the floor at the door to Great Grams' room and to sound the alarm if she tried to escape. Great Grams had already escaped several times.

That night, years of memories danced in my dreams, most of them good, but Great Grams had no good memories to sustain her. The last thing in the world I wanted was to have her sent to a nursing home; we had promised that would never happen. It wasn't her forgetfulness, but rather her insurmountable paranoia that affected every fiber of our lives. Certainly, it was understandable. If you can't remember moving an item, then someone else must have moved it. If you can't remember what your husband looked like, then perhaps he is that man that someone has snatched away. If you can't remember money in the bank, then all you are left with in life are the few dollars in your purse, and Great Grams held onto that purse day and night.

When I was a young child, my great grandmother had been my best friend. Almost ninety years my senior, she and I played together like brother and sister, sharing toys, and even vying for parental

Magnificent Kids!

affection. We shared an unusual relationship, each feeling responsible for the other. Afflicted with Alzheimer's disease, sometimes Great Grams was an adult. At those times, she advised me, protected me and expressed concern for me. At other times, I was the adult, watching her as we crossed the street, even "bubbie sitting" for her when my parents had to go out. I grew up embracing these responsibilities. As Great Grams became more child-like, I became a caregiver.

During the last year of her life, my great grandmother went in and out of several hospital dementia wards, most often for the urinary tract infections that so often accompany incontinence. When visiting her, I noticed that patients who were working on jigsaw puzzles seemed calmer than their frequently agitated peers. I went to the library to read about Alzheimer's disease and I learned that staying mentally active can help postpone the point at which an Alzheimer's patient is no longer functional in society.

After Great Grams passed away in 2007, I decided to collect jigsaw puzzles and distribute them to the facilities that had helped care for her. I contacted puzzle manufacturers and I placed collection bins in local libraries and businesses, and soon puzzles began to accumulate. Often, when I brought these puzzles to dementia facilities, I would stay a while and interact with the patients. It always gave me a good feeling to put smiles on their faces. Things were going so well that I decided to form a 501(c)3 organization, so that I could accept tax-free donations to cover the cost of shipping the puzzles to more distant facilities. I found that completing those 76 pages of forms was a daunting task for a twelve year old, but because of what I had experienced with Great Grams, I was determined to make a difference in the lives of as many Alzheimer's patients as possible.

In 2008, ***PuzzlesToRemember*** became a 501(c)3 organization and I began shipping puzzles, free, to dementia facilities. I soon realized that many of the puzzles that were being donated were not well-suited to the needs of Alzheimer's patients. Most had juvenile themes, and even adults with Alzheimer's are still adults who do not relate to puzzles about Sponge Bob and Dora. Many puzzles had too many pieces or pieces too small to be handled by this cohort. I decided to contact a puzzle manufacturer and plead my case for more appropriate puzzles and in 2010, **Springbok PuzzlesToRemember** were born. These puzzles have 12 or 36 large-sized, brightly colored pieces with memory-provoking themes. They have been widely praised as beneficial for Alzheimer's patients and they are being used in many Memory Cafes. I frequently receive photos of smiling faces, as Alzheimer's patients encounter an often elusive feeling of success. Since 2008, I have distributed over 30,000 puzzles, worth over $250,000, to over 2,300 Alzheimer's facilities around the world.

Because my family kept Great Grams at home with us, instead of sending her to a nursing home, I was confronted daily with her needs. I kept thinking about and reading about Alzheimer's disease. It was becoming clearer and clearer to me that I wanted to spend my life helping Alzheimer's patients and their caregivers. From age 8 to 10, I was assuming more and more responsibility for Great Grams. By the time I was 10, she was in and out of hospital geriatric wards. She, like 40 percent of individuals with Alzheimer's disease and dementia, was always trying to escape. I guess if someone doesn't recognize their surroundings and always think they are in an unfamiliar place, they are going to keep trying to escape and go home. That's what Great Grams did. However, this meant taking turns sleeping on the floor at the door to Great Grams' room. I spent many nights there. Great Grams wasn't just a wanderer as many Alzheimer's patients are, she was an escapist. She would actually plan her escapes, many times going to sleep with her underclothes and slip on under her nightgown so that she could make a faster escape. Once she actually did get out, early in the morning. In her 90's, with a bad leg, she made it down the hill, to the corner of a major street, flagged down a truck driver and told him we were trying to kill her. She convinced him to let her climb into the truck. Thankfully, he and his wife took her to the police station where she was, once again, admitted to the geriatric psychiatry ward.

Great Grams passed away when I was 10. Just months before her death, we took her to Hawaii with us. We had many wonderful experiences there, but also some harrowing ones. I used to joke that I got to meet many native Hawaiians on that trip. However, they were all members of the Honolulu Police Department. That's what happens when a woman in her 90's runs up to a Honolulu Policeman and tells him that those people are trying to kill her. Once someone says that, the police department is forced to investigate. Luckily the manager of the resort was going through similar episodes with her own mother. Great Grams passed away about seven months later. I'll always remember how difficult it was watching Great Grams lose her memories. It's something I don't want anyone to go through – ever. That's why I'm working so hard to change the face of Alzheimer's disease.

My journey as an Alzheimer's Researcher has been interesting. In 2009, someone at the 'Build a Bear Workshop' heard about my project and invited me to apply to become one of their huggable heroes. As a Huggable Hero, I was invited to St. Louis for an amazing experience. That's where I met some very inspirational young people, many of whom have remained my friends to this day. This trip included an amazing ceremony at the St. Louis Zoo, which was kept open in the evening for our private group, where we painted a mural for an inner city school in St. Louis. The 'Build a Bear Workshop' gave each winner a $2,500 check that could be donated to any charity of our choosing. ***PuzzlesToRemember*** was not yet a 501c3 organization, so I decided to donate my check to the Boston University Alzheimer's Disease center. I was invited to the Alzheimer's Disease Center, where I met some of the people that I work with to this day. It was a pivotal moment in my life.

On that first visit, I was invited to volunteer there during the following summer, when I turned 14. I was told that my work would be mostly clerical, and not glorious, but I would be around where Alzheimer's research was really happening. I spent the summer of 2010, typing endless names into the computer and carrying boxes up flights of stairs, but it was worth every minute of that for the few awesome opportunities I had. Soon, I was invited to attend a weekly journal club about Chronic Traumatic Encephalopathy, just as it was being discovered. I learned a great deal at those meetings, and I was treated like everyone else. Everyone else consisted of medical students, post-docs and researchers. I was even invited to the

Bedford Brain Bank, where I held in my hands the brain of an athlete who had died of CTE and I saw the destruction and how it was similar and also different from the destruction in Alzheimer's disease.

The Director of Boston University Alzheimer's Disease Center's Clinical Core, Dr. Robert Stern, had been honest with me. My job that summer had not been glorious. I kept working in the office until the following May when I was cleared to work in the lab. I was so happy when May finally arrived and I began my work in the Molecular Psychiatry and Aging Laboratory, where I work currently. My research covers various enzymes and their relationship to Amyloid Beta, a protein implicated in Alzheimer's disease. In particular, my research examines the effects of various peripheral and central ACE inhibitors on the risk of AD, and the correlation of ACE activity in the blood serum with that in the central nervous system. Several publications have already resulted from this work. Papers have been published in the Journal of Alzheimer's Disease, PLoS ONE, and in Molecular Psychiatry. I am also testing the effects of certain hormones on the buildup of Amyloid Beta and Tau. I gave poster presentations about my research at the 2013 American Association for Geriatric Psychiatry's annual conference and at the International Alzheimer's Association's 2013 conference. What I have found most wonderful about working on the Boston University School of Medicine campus is the apparent teamwork. World-famous researchers do data entry and even move boxes while an intern's ideas are met with interest, respect and encouragement.

For the past three years, I've been an editor for the AlzheimersReadingRoom.com, where I have the opportunity to interact with caregivers around the globe. Many times these caregivers ask me how to explain Alzheimer's to their young children. For this reason, I co-authored a book for children ages 4 through 9, hopefully explaining Alzheimer's disease at a level they can understand, while also providing them with some helpful coping skills. *"Why Did Grandma Put Her Underwear in the Refrigerator?"* is now available in English, German, French, Norwegian, Polish, Spanish and Chinese, soon to be followed by

Welsh, Italian, Hebrew, Tamil, and Sinhala. Fifty percent of the profits from these books goes to Alzheimer's causes.

As a result of my work, I have presented at conferences, had my efforts described in books, newspapers and magazines, appeared on TV shows, authored publications and presented many lectures. Currently, I am a junior neuroscience major at Boston University where I am on the Dean's List, after graduating from the Boston University Academy with Highest Honors. I am involved extensively in medical and social programs and have won many awards including the Jefferson Award for Public Service, the President's Call to Service Award, the Gloria Barron Prize for Young Heroes, Nestle's Very Best in Youth Award, The Presidential Volunteer Service Award (Gold Level), a Young Philanthropist Award, the Giraffe Hero Award, the Educational Research Center of America Community Contribution Scholarship, and the Diller Teen Tikkun Olam Award, among many others.

I have spent my life watching others, discerning their needs and trying to do my best to help them. But, I continually receive back much more than I could ever give. Knowing I put a smile on the face of someone who experiences only confusion and agitation is the greatest of rewards. I believe it is everyone's responsibility to reach out and make a difference. It doesn't have to be a huge, earth-changing event. Micro-philanthropy is the source of many wonderful advances. All you have to do is just one little thing to improve the life of someone else. No one is too young, too old, or too disadvantaged to make a difference in the world. Once you do this a few times, you will become addicted to the feeling of euphoria that comes with knowing you have made a difference.

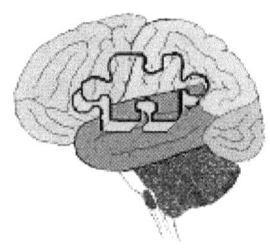

Max Wallack

What does the word 'magnificent' mean to you?

I think the word "magnificent" usually means very wonderful or very meaningful.

What do you give to the world?

I guess if I had to summarize it in one sentence, I would say that I try to give the world hope that we will be able to overcome Alzheimer's disease. I do this from many different perspectives, ranging from scientific research, to caregiver support, to therapeutic puzzles, to a book to help children understand this disease.

Why is this important to you?

I grew up as a caregiver to my Great Grandmother with this disease and I know how greatly this disease affects both patients and caregivers. I also realize the emotional costs of this disease to families as well as the huge economic costs to health care systems. With the number of cases growing steadily, the cost of this disease is an impending tsunami.

Why did you choose the project/idea that you did?

My great grandmother was in and out of nursing facilities during the last few months of her life. When I visited her there, I noticed that patients working on jigsaw puzzles seemed calmer and less agitated so I researched the effects of activities such as puzzles. Being an inventor and scientist at heart, I became interested in Alzheimer's research and I began working in a research lab when I turned 15. I recognized that there were no books that explained Alzheimer's disease to children in a way that was not dark or scary, and yet provided children with some useful coping mechanisms. That's why I wrote my book, *"Why Did Grandma Put Her Underwear in the Refrigerator? An Explanation of Alzheimer's Disease for Children."*

How old were you when you began your project?

I was 12 when I started *PuzzlesToRemember*, 15 when I began working in a research lab, and 17 when I wrote my book.

How did you go about getting it started?

I talked about this is my story.

Who is your project benefiting, and how?

More than 30,000 puzzles have been distributed to over 2,300 Alzheimer's facilities around the world. My book is receiving very positive feedback internationally and children are being helped. Articles I co-authored appeared in the American Journal of Alzheimer's Disease, on PLoS ONE, and in Molecular Psychiatry. I have several other papers under preparation. I am working with a hormone that is showing great promise as an early test for Alzheimer's, as well as a possible treatment.

Who were the key people that supported you, and how?

Early on, I was inspired by Jan Davidson. My colleagues and mentors at the Boston University Alzheimer's Disease Center, especially Dr. Qiu, Dr. Zhu, and Dr. Stern, continue to inspire me and support my efforts.

How much financial assistance did you have, and from whom?

I applied for 501c3 status so I could accept tax-free contributions. Several companies have supported my efforts with grants. American Express sends modest monthly checks that help with shipping costs. In lieu of royalties for my efforts in developing the *Springbok PuzzlesToRemember*, Springbok supplies me with a yearly allotment of puzzles and ships them to whichever facilities I choose. I have also received prize money from various sources, most of which I have donated for laboratory research.

How will you keep your project going into the future?

My book is doing well, and I may write another book in the future. The sales of the ***Springbok PuzzlesToRemember*** to individuals is quite successful, and I expect to continue directing people around the world as to where they can donate their used puzzles. My research is really just beginning. I am very optimistic about some of the results.

How have your peers responded to you setting up the project, and do they (or can they) get involved in any way?

My peers have been very supportive. Many help collect and deliver puzzles.

Do you see yourself as ordinary or extraordinary?

I see myself as an extraordinarily hard worker.

What is the most important thing to you?

Making a positive difference in the lives of others, with a focus on Alzheimer's disease.

What are your strengths?

I am hard working, loyal, a good friend and empathetic.

What are your weaknesses?

I am not a great athlete or artist.

Does your project require you to focus on your strengths?

For the most part, my project focuses on my strengths. Although, in writing my book, I had to stretch my artistic abilities.

Who is your greatest role model and why?

Jan Davidson because she taught me, when I was only 5, that if a person has the ability to help another person, then they have the responsibility to help.

Of all the people in the world, who inspires you the most?

I don't think I can narrow that down to one person.

How/where/why did you learn to care globally?

People everywhere have the same aspirations for health, happiness and freedom.

If you could change one thing in the world, what would it be?

For me personally, it would be to overcome Alzheimer's disease.

What do you think are the ingredients for success?

Passion about whatever you are involved in, Persistence, Empathy and Hard work

What is your global vision?

A more peaceful, less violent world, with less suffering from illness or injury.

What would be your message to the world?

Much more can be obtained by cooperation and listening than by competition and hostility.

If other kids wanted to start up their own magnificent project, what advice would you give them and what steps would you suggest they take?

Pick something you are very passionate about. Start small. Do just one little thing that benefits someone else. The feeling of euphoria you will get from helping others will spur you on to accomplish more.

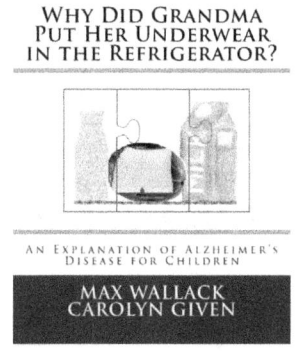

www.puzzlestoremember.org

"Children must be taught how to think, not what to think."
~ Margaret Mead

Nicholas Lowinger

    I started visiting homeless shelters at a young age and met children who laughed and played the way I did. I saw kids who were wearing shoes that were too big, too small or tattered, in deplorable condition and others without any footwear at all. Many children couldn't attend school because they had to share their footwear with another family member. I started donating my gently used clothing and shoes to the children and on one occasion, a small boy, who was barefooted, took a pair of my winter boots. Even though they were much too big for him, he was very happy just to have a pair of shoes to call his own, since he didn't have any at all. I felt sad that the boots did not fit him but I couldn't afford to buy new shoes for all of the children in the shelters. I knew then that at some point in my life I would provide new footwear for children in the shelters.

    In 2010, as part of a community service project for my bar mitzvah, I started the ***Gotta Have Sole Foundation*** so that I could donate brand-new footwear to children living in homeless shelters in the US. I contacted local schools, religious organizations, businesses and footwear manufacturers for footwear and monetary donations. At the same time, I called local shelters to introduce them to my program and to get the footwear orders for the children. After filling the orders, I delivered them personally to the children at the shelters. Over time, I reached out to shelters in other states so that I could help more children in need.

My project promotes equality and peace. The new footwear I donate to homeless children gives them the opportunity to attend school more regularly and to participate in sports and after-school programs alongside their peers. They are given equal opportunities and experience increased self-esteem. Recently, a teenage volleyball player was not going to be allowed to play in the state championships with her teammates because her sneakers were threadbare and held together with duct-tape. I donated the sneakers she needed so that she was able to participate. Her coach sent me a letter explaining how much the girl cried when she put on her new sneakers and how elated she was to be given this opportunity as she couldn't afford new ones. The sneakers allowed her to be included with her peers and to be treated equally. Whenever I return to the shelters with footwear for new children, I see children wearing the shoes and sneakers I previously donated to them and they come to greet me, hug me and show me that they are still wearing the footwear.

With the help of over 1,000 volunteers nationwide, I have provided new footwear for over 15,000 homeless children in 33 US states. My goal is to expand my program into all 50 states by the time I graduate from high school in 2016, so that all homeless children across the United States will have new footwear to call their own. When I donate footwear to children in shelters, I hand them out personally and help them to put them on. This gives me time to get to know them and listen to their stories.

Children have told me that they were unable to go to school because they lacked footwear, or if they did go, the kids in school would bully them because their footwear was in such a bad condition. Other children have told me that they couldn't participate in sports because they didn't have sneakers. These kids had low self-esteem, behavioral issues, and were doing poorly in school. They have expressed their gratitude, telling me how much they appreciate what I have done for them. There is no greater feeling for me than knowing that my efforts are helping needy children to have a better childhood and to feel equal.

My project is also about providing homeless children with the same opportunities as other children. A time during my project when I took a stand to help others was when a teenage boy and his mom fled a domestic abuse situation and arrived at a shelter with nothing but the clothes on their backs. They had to leave their domestic situation so quickly that the boy only had time to grab his mother's fur-lined boots. This was the footwear he had to wear to school and he was being ridiculed at school, not accepted by his peers and he became isolated and depressed. I bought him a pair of brand-new basketball sneakers and delivered them to him personally. He was overjoyed. Later that week, I received a call from the shelter worker saying that the sneakers helped lift the boy's self-esteem and that he was now more accepted by the kids at school.

One challenge I face is that the public doesn't understand the needs of homeless people. Many believe that because people are homeless, anything donated to them is better than nothing at all. Footwear donated to shelters is almost always used and in a poor condition. People don't realise that these shoes do not make children feel good about themselves, and that they could cause medical problems since they aren't the correct fit. I have given numerous presentations to schools, religious organizations, businesses and footwear manufacturers in order to try to change this mindset. An important part of my presentation includes an activity where participants switch shoes with a neighbor and are asked to notice what it feels like to wear shoes that don't fit them properly and are not of their choice. This experience has helped people understand the importance of new, properly fitting footwear that children can break in themselves, and that all people, regardless of whether or not they can afford a roof over their heads, deserve to be treated equally.

Because of the success of my footwear program for homeless children and because I saw a need to help other people in my community who were struggling financially, I started two new programs. One is for our nation's veterans who are living on or below the poverty line. It is called *SOLEdiers*. Through this program, I give veterans gift cards to footwear retailers so that they can purchase the footwear they need. I am proud to say that this program was established in honour of my grandfather who is a WWII veteran. I recently participated in an event for the veterans in my state and gave these gift cards to over 300 veterans. It was a privilege to thank these men and women for their service and for protecting my country's freedom. The other program I launched is called *Serving Love*, through which I donate sporting footwear to children from disadvantaged homes who want to play sports. Currently, I am working with a local non-profit organization that provides free tennis lessons and mentoring to children who cannot afford lessons. Combining my passion for equality and my love for tennis has been a perfect match. I hope to be able to expand both of these programs, nationwide.

There are many organizations which recognise and support youth for their volunteer work and peacemaking efforts, and I am honoured to have received the following awards:

2014 Charlotte Bacon Acts of Kindness Award
2013 Peace First Prize Fellowship - Peace First
2013 Muhammad Ali Humanitarian Award - Muhammad Ali Center
2013 CNN Hero Young Wonder
2013 Diller Teen Tikkun Olam Award - Helen Diller Family Foundation
2013 Kohl's Cares National and Regional Award Winner - Kohl's Cares Foundation (Kohl's Department Stores)
2013 Gloria Barron Prize for Young Heroes
2013 Youth Service Challenge 1st Place Winner - Jefferson Awards for Public Service
2013 Myra Kraft Community MVP Award - Kraft Family and Patriots Foundation
2013 Make A Difference Day Award - Points of Light Institute, Gannett and Newman's Own Foundation
2013 Global Teen Leader - We Are Family Foundation
2012 Presenter at BIF-8 Conference - Providence, Rhode Island
2012 Huggable Hero Award from Build-A-Bear Workshop Foundation

2012 Farm Rich Kids Who Give - Farm Rich Products
2012 Prudential Spirit of Community Award
2012 Presidential Volunteer Service Gold Level
2011 Jefferson Award for Public Service
2011 Hasbro Community Action Hero Award – Hasbro Toy, Inc. and GenerationOn
2011 Rainbow Award - Street Sights Magazine
2011 Youth Leader Award - Women's Center of Rhode Island

Lastly, youth volunteerism is something that is very important to me. I speak at numerous conferences and schools, encouraging youth to engage in service to their communities. I also mentor youth from around the globe. No one is too young to make a difference and I hope I am a positive role model for young people to see that they too can change the world. All it takes is an idea, passion, determination and encouragement.

What does the word 'magnificent' mean to you?

Something beautiful, striking

What do you give to the world?

I give the world hope for peace and equality for all people.

Magnificent Kids!

Why is this important to you?

I have met so many homeless children who are not treated the same way as people who have a roof over their heads. These kids are just like me, but their families have fallen on hard times. I don't believe that a person's financial circumstances should prevent them from being able to go to school and participate in sports and other activities with their peers. Every child deserves a childhood. Not enough people support these kids and it is important to me to be an advocate for them.

Why did you choose the project/idea that you did?

When I was five, I started to go to shelters with my mother. She wanted me to be more appreciative of everything I had. I met kids who were just like me, but their families had lost their homes. Some of them didn't have any footwear of their own and others had to share footwear with a sibling, which meant that they had to miss school when it wasn't their turn to wear the shoes. This distressed me and I knew I had to do something. After donating my used clothes and shoes and never being able to give the kids perfectly fitting footwear because we didn't wear the same size and because everyone wears their shoes in differently, I knew that at some point in my life I would donate new shoes to the kids.

How old were you when you began your project?

I was 11 when I created it and 12 when I launched it.

How did you go about getting it started?

My parents took me to get my project registered as a non-profit organization, and I spoke to schools, religious organizations and sent letters to footwear manufacturers. After I got some footwear and some monetary donations I contacted local shelters so they could give me their footwear orders.

Who is your project benefiting, and how?

My project benefits children in America who are living in homeless shelters (over 15,000 children in 33 states, so far). The new footwear gives them confidence, raises their self-esteem, allows them to go to school regularly and therefore do better in school, be accepted by their peers and participate in sports and social programs alongside them.

I also have a footwear program, ***SOLEdiers***, for our nation's military veterans who are living at or below the poverty line. I give them gift cards to footwear retailers so they can purchase new footwear for themselves and their families, thereby preserving their dignity.

In addition to my ***SOLEdiers*** program, I launched ***Serving Love*** as a third program. ***Serving Love*** is a program that gives sporting footwear to children from disadvantaged homes who want to play sports. I'm concentrating mostly on tennis right now, since tennis is one of my passions. I am fighting for the equality of homeless and disadvantaged children and our nation's military, living on the poverty line. These children deserve equal opportunities. The men and women who fought valiantly for America deserve our utmost respect and it is my turn to express my appreciation for everything they have done for my country.

Who were the key people that supported you, and how?

My parents and grandparents, footwear manufacturers, volunteer organizations, local universities and schools, my own school, friends and teachers, my temple and my community are key people who have supported me. People and corporations have sent footwear, held shoe drives and have contributed financially. Organizations involved with volunteerism such as the Jefferson Awards for Public Service, GenerationOn, We Are Family Foundation, Peace First Organisation, The Ali Center, and Diller Tikkun Olam, Gloria Barron, Kohl's Cares, Myra Kraft and the Patriots Foundation have also been extremely supportive, providing me with mentoring and financial support. There have also been a few celebrities, such as

Mark Wahlberg and Tony Danza, who have supported my program financially through their own foundations and by speaking about it.

How much financial assistance did you have, and from whom?

I rely a lot on financial assistance and have received it from various awards I have won for my volunteer efforts, from grants, corporations and private donors.

How will you keep your project going into the future?

I will always reach out to young people in my community and throughout the US as I feel it is very important that this project involve teens. This will hopefully make them more empathetic and help them understand the power that young people have to make a difference in the world. We can do anything if we have passion, an idea and the determination to turn that passion into action.

How have your peers responded to you setting up the project, and do they (or can they) get involved in any way?

My friends all respect what I am doing. Many of my friends and classmates volunteer whenever I have an event. They have been fully supportive.

Do you see yourself as ordinary or extraordinary?

I see myself as ordinary. All of this comes very naturally to me since I was raised in an environment where we have always done things for our neighbors, and other communities throughout the world, who are in need. I am very humble about what I do and I concentrate on serving others, which is far more important to me than any accolades I have received.

What is the most important thing to you?

The most important thing to me is equality of all people, and making a difference in their lives.

What are your strengths?

I am respectful of all people and do not judge anyone. I am a peacemaker. I have determination, passion, conviction and the understanding that I have the ability to create positive change in the world.

What are your weaknesses?

I am not as assertive as I should be, but I am getting better!

Does your project require you to focus on your strengths?

Yes, but it also requires me to focus on my weaknesses, because I have to speak to many people, and ask people for money. It has been a great learning process and an evolving experience.

Who is your greatest role model and why?

My greatest role model is my grandfather. He has always been very philanthropic, and he has always been very compassionate about others, putting their needs before his own. Through his business he hired "handicapable" people, recognizing their strengths and not their weaknesses. He gave them the opportunity to learn a trade and to work alongside able-bodied people. He helped them fit in during a time when other work programs kept them isolated from the workforce. My grandfather has given me advice on how to speak with presidents of corporations and how to raise funds to support my program. He is my biggest fan, and I am his!

Of all the people in the world, who inspires you the most?

The children I give footwear to inspire me the most. When I see the look of gratitude on their faces, and hear stories from them about what these new shoes will help them do, it makes me determined to reach more and more children all over the country.

How/where/why did you learn to care globally?

It first started from my family, who wanted me to be aware of how people all over the country and the world lived. They taught me that we have a responsibility to others who are less fortunate, and need to help them whenever we can. I also learned to care more globally when I received my first award, the Jefferson Award for Public Service, in 2011. The ceremony was in Washington, DC and I decided that whenever my family and I took a vacation or travelled anywhere for an award for my work, that I would contact a local shelter and bring along footwear for the children. At the ceremony, I met Sam Beard, the founder of the Jefferson Awards, who challenged me to be in 5 states and ship out 5,000 pairs of shoes to kids in the US within the next year. It was because of his push and confidence in me that I began to think on a more global level. By the way, I exceeded his and my expectations!

If you could change one thing in the world, what would it be?

If there was one thing I would like to change in the world it would be to change the mindset of all people with regards to equality. Everyone deserves equal opportunities and no one should be judged because of their differences. Peace is possible if we embrace and celebrate each other.

What do you think are the ingredients for success?

I believe the first ingredient for success is believing in yourself. Then you have to identify your passion, develop an idea, garner support, and finally, follow through with your idea by turning it into an action and knowing you can make a difference in the world.

What is your global vision?

My global vision is that all people, no matter what their race, religion, gender, ethnicity, sexual orientation or economic situation will be treated equally, with respect and dignity. I also envisage all children having a happy and fulfilling childhood, growing up with confidence and the knowledge that they can be or do anything that they desire. My hope is that young people will understand that they have the power to make a difference in the world, and create change.

What would be your message to the world?

My message would be to always believe in yourself and your ability to make a difference in the world, no matter what your age might be. It is never too early or late to make a difference. Youth should find something they are passionate about and turn their idea into a compassionate action.

If other kids wanted to start up their own magnificent project, what advice would you give them and what steps would you suggest they take?

I would applaud them, first of all, and encourage them to pick something that they can follow through with. I would tell them to make sure they have a support system in place. Their support person(s) do not have to be a parent, but can be anyone who would mentor them and help them get the project off the ground. I would also encourage them to get a group of friends to help, and to reach out into their communities for support. They could contact their local newspapers to have an article in the paper explaining what they have started. They should look for grants to apply for that could financially support their program. Also, it is very important to set realistic goals and what needs to be accomplished in a certain amount of time. Kids should create a plan of action, including meeting times, strategies for fundraising, and assign tasks so that everyone is contributing equally. Kids should also be able to recognize when they need the help of a mentor, and not be afraid to ask for help. Also, I would tell kids to make sure they are doing their project for the right reasons. If awards and recognition come their way, I encourage them to accept them humbly and to use the awards to further their projects. It is important to remain grounded.

http://www.gottahavesole.org

Olivia Bouler

My project is called *Olivia's Birds: Saving the Gulf*.

When I first heard about the oil spill, I was devastated. I grew up visiting the Gulf of Mexico's pristine beaches, spotting birds and feeding the dolphins. I knew it was nesting season and that danger was ahead especially for the brown pelicans that had just come off the endangered species list. The oil spill ruined the quality of life for thousands of birds, animals and people who live along the Gulf coast. I knew I had to do something - I couldn't just sit there, so I started my fundraiser, eventually raising $200,000 for Gulf recovery. I sent out 500 original drawings of birds to people who donated to several environmental organizations, especially the Audubon Society who were helping to clean up the Gulf of Mexico. People would send my mom their donation receipt and I would send them an original drawing. When the 500 were already accounted for, AOL helped send out prints of my work.

In the process, I have reached thousands of children in person, but many more thanks are due to the Public Service Announcement I did with Disney's 'Friends for Change'. My travelling exhibition of artwork and the book I wrote have spread the conservation message to people all over, but especially to children. Since then, I've written

Magnificent Kids!

and illustrated a bird guide for children, which also raises money for the Audubon Society.

The fundraiser started on May 3, 2010 and has been ongoing. Although I no longer send out drawings, I have been speaking to kids around the world about saving the planet and sharing my artwork with others. My goal is to raise money to help preserve animal habitats and to educate children about the importance of our environment. Money that I raised was used to establish a volunteer center for people who were there to clean the birds in Moss Point, Mississippi. By using social networking, I was able to spread the word about the fundraiser. I now have over 30,000 followers on my page where I continue to share drawings of birds, photos and conservation information.

I have learned that everyone has a talent to share and that we all need to work together to make the world a better place. I have also learned that the environment is in great trouble and we have to take habitat loss seriously. This experience has made me proud about setting a goal and working hard to meet it. I've been able to meet lots of great people who are working towards saving the environment, so I'm inspired to keep working on becoming an ornithologist.

I've been in many newspapers, magazines and on television shows around the world discussing ways that we can save the environment, appreciate birds and donate our talents to good causes. I've presented at many schools and at two TEDx conferences. I was on the White House Champion of Change panel and spoke at the Skirball Cultural Center in Los Angeles and for Roots and Shoots at New York University. The greatest moment had to be meeting President and Mrs. Obama.

In addition to my book, "Olivia's Birds", I am writing for the Huffington Post and have recently created an educational board game about bird migration. I am the 2011 winner of the Audubon Artist Inspiring Conservation Award, a Champion of Change by the White House and I was honored by Congressman Steve Israel as a Hometown Hero on August 31, 2010 and by TD Bank and the NY

Islanders in January 2011. I hosted my own White House Champion of Change round table discussion with environmental experts. I was selected as an honoree by Auburn University with a 2011 IQLA award, and was named ASPCA Kid of the Year. I was honored by the French newspaper Mon Quotidien and by AOL as one of their top 'feel good' stories of 2010, named Outstanding Stories of 2010 by My LI TV, and named Greatest Person of the day by The Huffington Post. I was named Dawn Junior Wildlife Champion, 2011 International Young Eco-Hero, and have received the Dale Earnhart Legends of Leadership Award. I am the winner of the 2011 Kohl's Cares Scholarship and the Gloria Barron Scholarship, and a semi-finalist in the Build a Bear workshop Huggable Heroes contest. A documentary about me won the 2012 MYHero award.

My story has appeared on many media outlets including: CNN, The Today Show, MSNBC, Larry King Live, People Magazine, The Mobile Press Register, The Guardian (UK), BBC radio, AOL News, Newsday, CBC, Independent, USA Today, The Disney Channel, *Time for Kids, Highlights, Scholastic,* and *American Girl* magazines, WKTU Cares, and the CBS Evening News with Katie Couric.

What does the word 'magnificent' mean to you?

Birds are magnificent creatures. They are amazingly engineered, from their hollow bones to their beautiful feathers.

What do you give to the world?

I have always loved birds. I painted the beauty of birds, hoping to show people that birds are worth saving. In the tradition of John James Audubon, painting the magnificent beauty of these winged creatures was my way of giving them a voice - telling people that birds are worth saving.

Why is this important to you?

I have learned that everyone has a talent to share and that we all need to work together to make the world a better place. I have also learned that the environment is in great trouble and we have to take habitat loss seriously.

Why did you choose the project/idea that you did?

When I heard about the oil spill, I was devastated. I wrote a letter to the Audubon Society saying I was 10 years old and willing to help. The only way I knew how was through my artwork.

How old were you when you began your project?

I was 10.

How did you go about getting it started?

By using social networking, I was able to spread the word about the fundraiser. I now have over 30,000 followers on my page. People would send my mom their donation receipt and I would send them an original drawing. When the 500 were already accounted for, AOL helped send out prints of my work.

Who is your project benefiting, and how?

Money I raised was used to establish an Audubon volunteer center for people who were there to clean the birds in Moss Point, MS. My goal has been to tell kids how they can help. I am achieving this through my books, artwork and class visits.

Who were the key people that supported you, and how?

Obviously my parents. I meet lots of kids who say they wanted to help but their parents told them to forget it. The people at Audubon were great, so was AOL, Sterling Publishing, my agent Marilyn and all of the ornithologists whom I met encouraged me to keep fighting for the cause. Bird nerds are really nice people and my facebook followers are super supportive and they really made it happen.

How much financial assistance did you have, and from whom?

My parents paid for the postage to mail all of my drawings, but AOL was a big help. They gave $25,000 to Audubon and then donated prints to keep the fundraiser going. I also received a Friends for Change grant from Disney to hand out copies of my book in Costa Rica.

How will you keep your project going into the future?

I am going to spend the rest of my life trying to help birds. I've had a one-person traveling exhibition of my artwork, which opened in 2012 at the Ned Smith Center in Pennsylvania and went to Cornell U and Corkscrew Nature Sanctuary in Naples, FL. I am going to work with more education programs using my book. I would love to continue to make birding videos and hopefully illustrate and write my next book about birds around the world. I currently write for the Huffington Post Teen section.

Magnificent Kids!

How have your peers responded to you setting up the project, and do they (or can they) get involved in any way?

No, my peers have not been supportive and at times I was teased about my work. It was hard to put up with it.

Do you see yourself as ordinary or extraordinary?

I always say if I can do it, anyone can. I'm an ordinary person who had a chance to do something extraordinary.

What is the most important thing to you?

My goal is to raise money to help preserve animal habitat and to educate children about the importance of our environment.

What are your strengths?

I am a good artist and I'm not afraid to express myself.

What are your weaknesses?

I'm messy and disorganized. I'm also super sensitive to criticism.

Does your project require you to focus on your strengths?

This experience has made me proud about setting a goal and working hard to meet it. I've been able to meet lots of great people who are working towards saving the environment.

Who is your greatest role model and why?

I have always loved the work of John James Audubon. His paintings showed the beauty of birds, which is why I decided to share paintings, hoping to show people that birds are worth saving. I was also inspired by the work of Rachel Carson, who proved that one person can truly make a difference. Without her book *Silent Spring*, DDT use would have continued and the bald eagle would surely be extinct.

Of all the people in the world, who inspires you the most?

I am really inspired by all the scientists I've met. Scott Weidensaul, Steve Kress, Melanie Driscoll are all people trying to save birds. But honestly I was really star struck when I met President Obama.

How/where/why did you learn to care globally?

My parents encouraged me to do something about the things in the world I want to change. They also shared their love of nature with me, taking me hiking in Ireland, setting out bird feeders and swimming in the Gulf of Mexico.

If you could change one thing in the world, what would it be?

I would make mean people nice.

What do you think are the ingredients for success?

Children still believe they can make a difference and that makes them more likely to be successful. Adults find too many reasons not to do something, so I'd say kids know something grownups don't.

What is your global vision?

Countries around the world should commit to not only protecting current habitats, but also restoring those that we have polluted. It can be done. By protecting tracts of land, we can make wildlife corridors or flyway zones, maximizing the habitat birds and animals need. By curtailing pesticide use, we can reduce chemicals found in our marshes, streams and oceans. And by working together, our world can stop the changes in our climate.

Magnificent Kids!

What would be your message to the world?

Can you imagine a world without birds chirping and flying overhead, or an ocean without sea turtles gliding along, or coral reefs that turn grey and die? When we talk about quality of life, the benefits of our natural habitat are immeasurable for animals and humans alike. We need to work together to make sure future generations have the opportunity to experience nature.

If other kids wanted to start up their own magnificent project, what advice would you give them and what steps would you suggest they take?

Every one of us has a great gift we can use to help the earth. Everyone, at any age, can do something, whether it is picking up trash along the side of the road, filling a bird feeder or bringing reusable bags to the grocery store. For me, I used my artwork. From caterpillars to cancer, find your cause and use your talents. It might start small, but who knows who you will inspire. Every little bit counts.

www.oliviabouler.net

Olivia Wright

My name is Olivia and I am just a normal 15 year old who loves acting, singing, theatre, playing chess, writing poetry and stories, and volunteering. I stay busy like so many of my peers. I have a wonderful family who supports my dreams and my organization ***H.U.G.S.*** and friends I get to volunteer with. What makes me a little different is that unlike most teens my age, I spend many hours running my organization, ***Tennessee H.U.G.S. (Help Us Give Shoes)***. We collect gently used shoes from others through shoe drives, people bringing me shoes or I collect them, and some people even mail shoes to me. It is nothing to come home and see 6 or 7 boxes on my front porch from people in North Dakota, Florida, or anywhere.

When I began ***H.U.G.S.*** I had a small goal and as I collected and then gave the shoes away to kids who needed them, we began to count for fun. We began sharing shoes here in the U.S.A. then people we knew were going on trips where there was a need for shoes and so we sent shoes internationally. Then disasters struck around us like the Tennessee Flood, Tuscaloosa, AL tornados and the Earthquake in Haiti. We showed up to help and give shoes and sent boxes of shoes to Haiti. Thinking of kids and just people in general wearing shoes that may have otherwise been thrown away or re-sold makes me happy.

When I was younger, I spent a lot of time worrying about other people, especially children, and how I could help others. I worried about children who were sick, so I became involved with the Ronald McDonald House and the Leukemia and Lymphoma Society, as well as other such organizations. I always felt I could do more though, instead of just showing up for what other people had started. When I was 9, my mom and I were watching an episode of a show called 'Feed the Children' and I heard that children don't have all their basic needs like food, clothes and shoes. Well, I thought, I have shoes and I know others with lots of shoes and we can give them to other kids who need them. *H.U.G.S.* was born.

On our first shoe drive we collected 670 pairs of shoes and to date *H.U.G.S.* has sent over 43,000 pairs of gently used shoes to places such as the Appalachian Mountain regions, Russia, Brazil, Dominican Republic, Liberia, Uganda and disaster areas including those hit by Haiti's earthquake and Hurricane Sandy. I use my voice to encourage other teens to get out into their communities and volunteer and also to speak for the children in the world - some right here in the U.S., who do not have simple things like shoes. I love to show others what they can do to help - sometimes it simply means just cleaning out your closet!

H.U.G.S. has been recognized with honors and awards including Sumner County's Most Influential Top 30 (Sumner Co. Tennessee), Hendersonville Optimist Club Over and Beyond Award, National American Miss Volunteer Award, International Jr. Miss Volunteer, Governor Bill Haslem State of TN Governor's honor, Kohl's Cares Store and Regional Winner, Build a Bear Huggable Hero finalist, Mary Catherine Strobel finalist (Nashville), Generation Hero 2013 Hero, 2013 Kids are Heroes award and Three Dot Dash global teen leader award.

Some people would like me to believe I am too young to make a difference, but I know that kids my age CAN make a difference. I have also learned that giving is its own reward. I just want to show others how they, too, can change the world. Everyone can make a difference!

What does the word 'magnificent' mean to you?

Oh, wow! Magnificent means something that is excellent. It means bigger than life and amazing in every way possible. I certainly do not consider myself magnificent although I don't mind people thinking that *H.U.G.S.* is. I do love to encourage other kids to be magnificent and the best they can be!

What do you give to the world?

Not only do I give shoes, my time and my energy to others, but I also give a BIG piece of my heart! I want to show other people that someone really cares about them enough to do big things for them. I really enjoy sharing my joy for life and encouragement with others who may not have it. It is amazing what ONE pair of shoes can bring to another person. It is also amazing to see my friends share their joy of giving as they help me with *H.U.G.S.* People who do shoe drives for us get to share their hearts too. I think giving goes alongside happiness and it can be contagious!

Magnificent Kids!

Why is this important to you?

Giving is something I think we should ALL do. I think if everyone were more selfless, the world would be a better place. I feel like God has blessed me so much, I just want to give back.

Why did you choose the project/idea that you did?

Well, when I was watching 'Feed the Children' that night, I knew I wanted to make the lives of children missing things that I take for granted every day, better. Food is important and so is clothing, but I also knew shoes were something kids needed to protect their feet from diseases, weather conditions, cuts and bruises and to make them happier (we get REALLY cute shoes given to us!). I talked with my parents and we all agreed that shoes were something that most people had to give without even going to Walmart!

How old were you when you began your project?

9 years old

How did you go about getting it started?

My parents helped me come up with the name on a long road trip. We wrote about 100 names. ***H.U.G.S.*** was my favorite. Then I cleaned my own closet, asked my youth group director at church to do a shoe drive and on the first one, we collected 670 pairs of shoes. Then by word of mouth, my speaking to groups, schools, churches and others, we just grew and kept collecting shoes! We now have ***H.U.G.S.*** organizations in other states and individuals who do annual shoe drives.

Who is your project benefiting, and how?

We benefit anyone who can't afford their own decent pair of shoes. We give shoes to men, women and children in the U.S.A. and many countries around the world. Shoes have been delivered to inner cities like Nashville, carried to the Appalachian Mountains, sent and given in Haiti, Dominican Republic, 2 places in Africa, Russia, Brazil and Mexico. We take ANY kind of shoe, as well as coats, socks, mittens and just about anything that will help people's wellbeing.

Who were the key people that supported you, and how?

My family, my church youth group including the directors and parents, my community and city of Hendersonville including many neighbors and my school. I have friends I've met from all around America, some through acting and singing and some through pageantry over the past 9 years. People are wonderful and so willing to help when they are asked!

How much financial assistance did you have, and from whom?

Right now we do not take any financial assistance. We have been given gift cards for gas to deliver shoes, but mostly I raise the money myself or my family contributes. We plan on becoming a non-profit by this summer. Honestly, we collect shoes which are free and sitting in other people's closets, just waiting for new homes.

How will you keep your project going into the future?

I plan on making *H.U.G.S.* a non-profit but it's simple as I will always ask people to give and host shoe drives. People will always have a need for this basic necessity. I hope to build an orphanage or school through *H.U.G.S.* soon. I have a strong, supportive family who will always help me.

How have your peers responded to you setting up the project, and do they (or can they) get involved in any way?

Oh, yes! People are always asking to help *H.U.G.S.* They know when they give we will never sell their shoes like some organizations do. We take them and give them straight to new owners in need. I have schools and churches asking to do shoe drives, missionaries asking to deliver shoes, friends and peers across the U.S. starting their own ***H.U.G.S.*** organizations (for instance, Cleveland H.U.G.S. Mississippi H.U.G.S. Louisiana H.U.G.S. and Alabama H.U.G.S.). We have one awesome girl, Macie Roberts, who has collected thousands of shoes!! She is relentless when it comes to collecting shoes and has a big heart for others. She is a true hero!

Do you see yourself as ordinary or extraordinary?

Oh, I see myself as ordinary. I just do what every teen my age can do. I want to show others they can do ANYTHING like this. But you can't just talk. You have to actually do it, too!

What is the most important thing to you?

I know that I am important because I am a role model and I take that very seriously. I am often in the public eye and I know that in a world where lots of teens my age are acting crazy to get attention or further their careers, I think it's important young kids/teens have role models who keep a clean profile and are doing things to make a difference.

What are your strengths?

I am a people person and I love all people. I never stop seeking others to help, even if it's just sharing a smile or being there for them. I do think I'm a good leader and can always see ways to help.

What are your weaknesses?

I am always late and I want to 'save the world' so sometimes I take on too many things.

Does your project require you to focus on your strengths?

Definitely! If I didn't lead and people didn't see my passion, I think *H.U.G.S.* probably would never get shoes.

Who is your greatest role model and why?

I have so many role models - most of them women including my mom. My daddy is a great role model to me too. My greatest role model is a woman who helped me start *H.U.G.S.* though. Her name is Maria Duvall. She showed me that not only can you do anything you dream of, you can also do more! She has 3 or 4 small businesses, is the first college graduate (with honors!) from her family and never stops. She inspires girls all over the U.S.A. and just became the founding principal of D.C.'s newest elementary prep school. She not only believes in making a difference, she DOES and never stops! Another role model is Janet Ivey-Duensing who has an organization called Janet's Planet. Her dream is for kids to learn her love of space. I like to see women just like me who are making a difference.

Of all the people in the world, who inspires you the most?

Right now I am most inspired by every day heroes. Macie Roberts, who has collected thousands of shoes for *H.U.G.S.* inspires me. We never ask her. She just shows up with hundreds of shoes all sorted and tied. She is amazing! I am also inspired by Dianne Sawyer because I want to be like her one day, reporting the news.

How/where/why did you learn to care globally?

I believe it was instilled in me from a very young age. My mom and dad both grew up poor and are always thinking of others all around the world. My little brother is from a Russian orphanage and I've seen how that can be. I'm very mission minded.

Magnificent Kids!

If you could change one thing in the world, what would it be?

It may sound silly, but to know that all children had a loving family would make my life complete. Until then, I'll just give shoes.

What do you think are the ingredients for success?

A caring heart, a driving desire to lead and show others how to lead and help, and surrounding yourself with people who can help you and teach you.

What is your global vision?

To collect and deliver shoes to as many places as possible with all the resources we have. One day, I will not have school to worry about and will be able to focus more on helping others. I do want to build an orphanage or school when I am 17!

What would be your message to the world?

People care enough to give you shoes. You are loved!

If other kids wanted to start up their own magnificent project, what advice would you give them and what steps would you suggest they take?

You can do anything. Be assertive and be relentless sharing your passion. Let your passion be contagious! Do it for the real reason of helping others and not for your own glory. Encourage other kids like us to help and be magnificent!

www.tennesseehugs.org

Samuel Lam

Strumming my fingers on the Yixing teapot before me, I glanced down at my watch. In fifteen minutes, I would be discussing cyber safety with a board of administrators and student representatives at Beijing University. Shifting in my seat, I smiled, thinking back to my first presentation earlier that year on "cyberbullying" and youth leadership in front of a hundred middle school students at Friends Academy in New York. My cheeks had turned bright red as students gathered around me to share their own experiences with cyberbullying and to inquire into how they could get involved.

"Stop picking on him! He just came from China and doesn't speak English well."

In eighth grade, I had stood up to Bradley, a bully who had been ridiculing Richard's broken English and outdated style of dress for weeks. Soon, I found myself the target of Bradley's attacks, both at school as well as online. Bradley and his friends plastered my Facebook wall with vitriolic statements and racial slurs and when I tried to un-friend them, they paid other students to post hateful comments on my wall instead. At the time, I had no idea who to turn to for help. Lost, humiliated, and defenseless, I felt caught in a seemingly hopeless battle. The event was a difficult one, but it became the catalyst and inspiration for me to co-found the **End to Cyber Bullying (ETCB) Organization**.

Convinced that there was a need for online resources to assist students facing similar assaults, I created a modest website to post information on cyberbullying statistics and preventative measures. However, I quickly realized that so much more needed to be done. Inspired, I reached out to and enlisted the help of my classmates. Our grassroots movement gained momentum and raised awareness, while strongly advocating for youth leadership and character development. Ironically, we utilized the same social media, not to tear and break each other down, but to promote and connect to youth. One person told a few friends, those friends told a few others and soon word began to spread exponentially - and just like that, the **End to Cyber Bullying Organization (ETCB)** was officially born.

It started off as a simple, high school project in ninth grade with a belief that we could produce social change. That belief triggered a global awareness campaign and has since developed into one of the largest youth-driven initiatives in the world. *ETCB* has grown into a 501(c)(3) not-for-profit and has triggered a global awareness campaign uniting over 4.5 million individuals internationally. With over 1,200 volunteers, *ETCB* has established initiatives in not just the US, but also in nations such as China, Great Britain, and Australia. Partnering with other organizations such as the Girl Scouts of USA and Sears Anti-Bullying Coalition has enabled us to expand even further. All of the money raised has been utilized to continue expanding *ETCB*, helping to increase the impact we've made. I'm humbled to have had the opportunity to work with Senator Jeffrey Klein and Miss New York and to have appeared on national CBS2News and GBTV. But most importantly, I am grateful to have been able to help and offer comfort to over 2,500 cyberbullying victims of all ages. Future victims no longer need to feel as isolated and helpless as I once did.

Because cyberbullying is such a modern phenomenon, it can be difficult for lawmakers and adults in the community to tackle the issue. Suicide cases, like those of Tyler Clementi and Amanda Todd, call for the direct involvement of youth. Especially with cyberbullying, it is imperative to start at the root of the issue: the mentality and belief that it is okay, or almost "cool" to hurt or attack another individual online. Worse yet, many people turn an apathetic ear to the issue. What they don't realize is that millions of kids, and even adults, across the world are victims of online harassment.

Perhaps the greatest obstacle I have faced in working with youth is doubt as to whether we can make a real difference in the world. Under social and even parental pressure, I've struggled to determine what it is I want to achieve, let alone overcome the scepticism that I *can* achieve these goals. I hope **ETCB** will present to the youth across the world, the message that our generation has the capability and power to solve many of the world's conflicts. But only when we band together can we and will we make a difference. Too often, young people leave making a difference to the future. Only in the heat of the moment did I recognize that I could do something right now.

The words the cyber bully had said to me echoed faintly in my mind as I entered the conference room, but in a way, I felt fortunate that those very words had brought me here. Taking a deep breath, I greeted the audience: "Regardless of your mission, remain true to your personal beliefs and you may be surprised about just how much you can accomplish."

My accomplishments include being awarded the Gold Medal – Congressional Award (2011/12), the President's G.H.W. Bush's Volunteer Service Award – Point of Light Award (2012), President Obama's Volunteer Service Award (2012) and the Prudential Very Best in Youth Award – New York State Honouree (2012). I was also a finalist in the Nestle Very Best Youth Award (2012), and a semi-finalist in the Huggable Hero Award (2012).

Magnificent Kids!

In 2008, my grandfather was diagnosed with prostate cancer. This event was a major turning point for me and a key inspiration for me to volunteer, to help others and to positively benefit and impact my community. Since then, I've raised over $250,000 for cancer research and have been awarded various community and volunteer awards. Though I am currently a Senior at Jericho Senior High School, after careful deliberation, I've decided to take a year off in between high school and my studies at Harvard College.

I have realized that my time as a youth is limited and that I must strive to pursue my passions and heart felt goals - **End to Cyber Bullying**. With all the incredible support from our employees, volunteers, as well as generous contributions from donors across the world, I truly believe that ***ETCB*** can start a movement that will make the world tremble. During my year off, I will be working and dedicating my energies and time to growing and expanding ***ETCB*** - from revamping and creating the largest and most comprehensive online database, to managing a team of professional and trained online psychologists and responders to assist in cyber bullying cases. I will conduct and fund additional research on bullying, cyber bullying and the psychological states of victims/bullies, as well as share my story to schools and colleges across the globe. Social media is the key to uniting teens from all across the world under one banner. Why not devote this short life to service - a journey where we help others become catalysts for positive social changes. You can find out more about what I'm up to at www.samuelklam.com.

What does the word 'magnificent' mean to you?

To me, magnificent means something that one wouldn't normally expect. It's out of the ordinary and it transcends societal expectations and norms. To be magnificent, means to stand out; because of your actions, because of your beliefs and because you dare to achieve what others wouldn't.

What do you give to the world?

I feel as if I serve as a reminder to youth, parents and educators internationally that cyberbullying is a pressing issue in today's society. I accentuate my skill set, strengths, abilities and time, to make a difference in the world, especially by highlighting cyberbullying and attempting to correct a very important issue.

Why is this important to you?

Cyberbullying has been a personal issue for me in the past. Many of my friends, family members, family friends, (and millions of others), have been seriously affected by cyberbullying. With the increasing use of technology, it's important that we learn how to safely use technology online.

Additionally, I think it's critical that youth embodies the belief that they can make a difference in the world. It really comes down to mindset and pure willpower to think that you can make a visible and lasting change in those around you. Everyone has the power to make a difference in someone's life and it's important that young people realize the strength and power of this ability.

Why did you choose the project/idea that you did?

As I mentioned in the previous question, Cyberbullying has been a personal issue for me in the past. Many of my friends, family members, family friends, (and millions of others) have been seriously affected by cyberbullying. With the increasing use of

Magnificent Kids!

technology, it's important that we learn how to safely use technology online.

How old were you when you began your project?

After I was cyberbullied in 8th grade, I started to work on cyberbullying awareness and prevention. I was 13 at the time.

How did you go about getting it started?

At first I created a simple site as well as doing a lot of research online. To educate myself, I read through statistics, research journals and articles regarding cyberbullying. After creating the website, I started to inquire the help of my friends and classmates around me. Word really spread and things started to move faster and faster as more people became involved in the growth and drive of *ETCB*.

Who is your project benefiting, and how?

My project is benefiting students, parents, educators, adults and individuals worldwide. www.endcyberbullying.org serves as a consortium that drives tens of thousands of visitors per month. We've helped over 2,500 cyberbullying victims who have reached out to us and we've impacted over 4.5 million people worldwide. We serve to spread awareness about cyberbullying, educate individuals, as well as to inspire youth and educators to take a more active role against cyberbullying. We have initiatives springing up across the world.

Who were the key people that supported you, and how?

When it comes to key people, the organization was completely backed and funded by youth. I didn't have the support of mentors, nor parents, nor adults. My only support was found in my peers and youth, whose ideas and actions have become instrumental to *ETCB*'s success. The Executive Board of *ETCB* is made up of individuals who are action oriented and who dream big. They're extremely dedicated to the cause and it's inspiring to work alongside individuals who are changing the world and loving each and every moment of it.

How much financial assistance did you have, and from whom?

None - ***ETCB*** was completely self-funded. We relied on fundraisers, private donations and sponsorships.

How will you keep your project going into the future?

ETCB operates on the basis that youth lead their movement in their respective society. Though I'm 18 currently, I feel as if I'll always be a kid at heart and personally, I'd always want to have a role in ***ETCB***, especially since it's such an important topic to me. The project will continue growing because of the number of individuals who continually join the movement. They are the heart and voice of ***ETCB*** and without them, word would not spread so rapidly. It's honestly inspiring to see so many people come together from all different nations and work together towards our common goal - to end cyberbullying.

How have your peers responded to you setting up the project, and do they (or can they) get involved in any way?

My peers have been extremely responsive to the idea. The faculty were very welcoming as well when ***ETCB*** started and many of the staff were extremely accommodating (especially when we were making progress in my high school). Peers have been contacting us from all across the world and the US is just one of several countries getting involved and volunteering to head their own ***ETCB*** initiative in their respective regions.

Do you see yourself as ordinary or extraordinary?

I see myself as an ordinary person, who had the right mindset, luck and opportunity to be able to accomplish some extraordinary things.

Magnificent Kids!

What is the most important thing to you?

Family, friendship, commitment and passion in the work that you do.

What are your strengths?

Leadership, charisma, ambition, dedication, passion and intelligence.

What are your weaknesses?

My youth turned out to be both a weakness and strength. Weakness in that I certainly wasn't the most experienced leader. I had basic knowledge on business plan development, accounting and financial book keeping - but I had a huge desire to learn. I think that being a youth helped me to gain the attention of the media and my peers because other young people were able to connect and relate to me.

Does your project require you to focus on your strengths?

Yes my project requires me to focus a lot on leadership, communication skills, project management, business development and long-term strategies. Though I'm young, I'm a very friendly, energetic and goal-oriented individual. I set practical milestones for the company to reach and I'm very careful when it comes to allocating funds towards each department's growth for *ETCB*. I love working alongside individuals, hearing their feedback and ideas and putting ideas, minds and people together to grow a cause.

Who is your greatest role model and why?

My oldest brother Chris, who is now a Senior in the Brown PLME Combined Medical Program, has proven to be one of my greatest role models. He is a paragon of moral integrity and he is guided by his values of love, family and humanity. Last summer, he spent one month in China helping HIV-afflicted children at an orphanage in Henan. Despite his busy schedule, Chris spent one month without the comforts and commodities that many of us take for granted in the

US: no cell phone, TV, Wi-Fi, electronics, clean drinking water or spacious living quarters.

This year, after much reflection, Chris announced his withdrawal from the prestigious PLME program to instead pursue his passion of studying gender equality or child development. Instead of becoming a doctor, he hopes to become a professor, psychologist or even an elementary school teacher one day - a career path that he feels will enable him to better impact and help the lives of others.

I think that especially in today's society, young people are pressured to conform to society's expectations. It is difficult for an individual to be mature enough to look into himself and figure out what it is that truly makes him happy, without society's ideals influencing his decision. In Chris, I see an individual on whom I would like to model myself, and like him, be a person who's actions speak louder than words. Likewise, I hope that I will be able to look into my heart and ascertain for myself what it is that I truly want.

Of all the people in the world, who inspires you the most?

Again... my brother Chris.

How/where/why did you learn to care globally?

I've been an active volunteer from a very early age. My grandfather was diagnosed with cancer when I was in middle school, which moved me to volunteer with the American Cancer Society and volunteer my time helping out at various cancer clinics. I served as patient navigator and liaison and helped schedule cancer patient education workshops. Since middle school, I've taken on larger leadership roles and I started planning and hosting my own fundraisers and events to raise money for cancer. I conducted my own independent study, studying the psychological symptoms and quality of life in cancer patients. My research won me various rewards such as becoming an Intel STS Semifinalist, 1st Place Research Association Science Fair, 2nd Place New York State Science & Engineering Fair and various others. Since the time my grandfather was diagnosed with cancer, I've helped raise over $250,000 towards additional cancer research.

Much of the success attributed to **ETCB**, I've learnt through helping out at the American Cancer Society. This experience fostered my leadership, event coordination, public speaking and people skills. Volunteering has helped me to develop a keen sense of application and awareness that action is needed not just on a community level but on a global one.

If you could change one thing in the world, what would it be?

I would change the mentality of our youth today. I am referring to the belief that we are too young to accomplish certain things, or that our youth prevents us from making a real and lasting impact on our society.

What do you think are the ingredients for success?

As clichéd as it may seem, the recipe for success is for young people to pursue their dreams and never give up. The only mistake one could make is not trying to help others. Even more, if you are motivated by passion and a genuine concern for a cause, you will succeed regardless of your age. Find that one thing that you love and see how you can hone in on your skills and cultivate expertise around you to accomplish your goal. Regardless of your mission, remain true to your personal beliefs and be receptive to those around you. You may even be surprised at just how much you can achieve.

What is your global vision?

An international teen movement, united and empowered to make a global, national and local impact.

Samuel Lam

What would be your message to the world?

I think that especially in society today, young people are pressured to conform to society's expectations. It is hard for an individual to be mature enough to look into yourself and figure out what it is that truly makes you happy without society's ideals influencing your decision. This is something that I battle with every day. Is what I want, what my parent's, my friend's or what society wants, or is it truly what I want? I know it is incredibly hard to ask youth to make that decision, but ultimately I would tell them to look into their hearts and see for themselves what they truly want.

If other kids wanted to start up their own magnificent project, what advice would you give them and what steps would you suggest they take?

For immediate advice to those individuals that want to help, I would say dream big. Whatever you're doing, whether you're ending cyber bullying or ending cancer, you have to believe what you are doing is right and you have to love it. Better yet, it is important to find other people who share your passions and interests and to join with them to help better our world. Everyone can find their niche to fill; everyone can find some way to help others and to take on a cause that will have a positive impact on our planet. Individually we are like a small blade of grass but together we can be seen from miles away.

www.endcyberbullying.org

"It is easier to build strong children
than to repair broken men."
~ Frederick Douglass

Shekhar Kumar

Hello! My name is Shekhar Kumar and I am a Grade 11 International Baccalaureate student at Turner Fenton Secondary School in Brampton, Ontario. For the past three years, I have immersed myself in community service, student leadership, youth advocacy and social activism.

In 2003, when I was six years old, my family and I emigrated from India to Canada. Despite both of my parents having Bachelor degrees, my parents were employed at the minimum wage and for a few years, my family lived in one of the worst neighbourhoods in Scarborough. Eventually, my parents' jobs improved slightly and we moved to a better suburb of Toronto. The reason I'm mentioning this is to share with you, where I have come from and how my unique perspective has affected the activities that I am part of.

It was at this time that I began being exposed to what Canada was really like - the vast variety of intermingling cultures and backgrounds. At the same time, I also discovered that some places, including my neighbourhood, had many problems. Gangs, violence and drugs were very open, even to a middle school student like me. I also began to experience certain forms of racism and bullying. I was regularly victimized because of my skin colour and heritage. Then we bought our first house in Brampton, which is where I am now. I had always done well at school, so I enrolled as a student in the International Baccalaureate Programme, an enriched program for motivated students.

It was also at this time that I realized that through social service, I could overcome the racism and bullying that I had endured. I became involved in politics by interning at my Member of Parliament's office. I served as an advisor to the Ontario Minister of Education and I volunteered with the Brampton's Mayor Youth Team and Free the Children. I also became a cadet at my local Royal Canadian Air Cadets squadron and founded a charity to collect shoes for those who require them - **Shoes to End Poverty (STEP)**. In one year, we have collected 900 pairs of shoes, raised $3,000 and have been featured on local television.

Regarding my internship with my local MP, I assisted in the development of Bill C-394, an enactment that amends the Criminal Code to make it an offense to recruit, solicit, encourage or invite a person to join a criminal organization whilst also establishing a penalty for the offence and a more severe penalty for the recruitment of persons less than eighteen years of age. My background really increased my ability to share my ideas with the MP.

In terms of **STEP**, my main project, we have online outreach via Facebook to more than 1,500 young people in the community and we have had a total outreach of more than 600,000 people across four newspapers in two countries, collected over 900 pairs of shoes and raised in excess of $3,000.

Some of my key accomplishments include assisting in the development of Bill C-394 (41-1), outreach via social media to 6,000 individuals about social and political issues, advocating for youth involvement in politics on Rogers TV to an audience of more than 100,000 viewers, and recognition in Canada's House of Commons by Kyle Seeback, MP for contributions to community service in Brampton.

I have also run the collection of 2,234 non-perishable food items (558.5 kilograms) for Free the Children at my school, and 300 books for the United Way of Peel Region. Furthermore, I have logged 900 volunteer hours (23 times more than the amount required to graduate from an Ontario high school). I have received awards including Brampton's Best Junior Citizen Award (recognized two years in a row by a local newspaper for commitment to community service), Top Junior State of America Speaker and a Youth Summer Program Scholarship valued at $1,225.

In the past three years of being heavily involved in my community, I have learned that volunteering and social service are pursuits that bring together people from different religions and cultures all over the world. I made many friends and learned about how great an impact a person like me can have on the lives of others.

What does the word 'magnificent' mean to you?

I believe that "magnificent" can mean a variety of things - but that it is up to you to determine what being magnificent truly consists of. To me, for example, magnificent can mean go-getting for excellence, setting a bar for myself that I want to achieve and having the ability to inspire others to strive for something bigger than themselves.

Magnificent Kids!

What do you give to the world?

In most of my extracurricular activities, I try to consider the global implications. For example, with ***Shoes To End Poverty***, I understand that giving back to my community by providing a resource that many people lack, might inspire someone else in the world to take part in a similar activity, or it may inspire that individual to get involved in his/her own cause or initiative. This feeling of being able to encourage others to make a meaningful impact on our world is something that drives me to keep up my dedication and commitment to social service.

Why is this important to you?

This is extremely important to me because I understand the fundamental impacts that one can have by giving back. Coming from an immigrant family that arrived in Canada with very little, the organizations and support groups which helped my family to become established, had an indelible impact on how I perceive people who work for their communities. Learning from my experiences, I began applying myself in similar scenarios and started to participate in community service and volunteering.

Why did you choose the project/idea that you did?

I chose to start ***Shoes To End Poverty*** (abbreviated STEP), in March 2012. Having been a volunteer with various programs before, I chose to assist at the Toronto's annual 10K Marathon. While volunteering in the core of downtown Toronto, I began to realize how fortunate I truly was. I remember thinking, "There were the extremely wealthy, and then there were homeless people living in abject poverty. This is so wrong! Why is it that some people have nothing to eat for dinner, whereas others have resources in abundance?" After this realization, an image struck me and it hasn't yet left my mind.

While handing out water to the runners/contestants, I saw a man without shoes; he was only in socks. The temperature that day was pretty chilly; 0 degrees C, at least. This man was around 50 years old, with no home and practically no money. Basically, he lacked all of the things that we deem to be necessities. Inspired by this man's tough circumstances, I vowed to try to correct this problem. I contacted my friends to create a group of students who felt compelled to reduce the growing poverty in our communities. The fact that the elderly man didn't have shoes impacted me the most. I said to my friends: "I look at this guy without shoes, and then I look at myself, and my friends who just throw out shoes that get a little ripped. Most people do not make any attempt to donate, sell or even try to fix their 'worn-out' shoes." And that's the story of how *STEP* came to be.

How old were you when you began your project?

I founded *STEP* in March 2012, so I was a little more than fifteen years old.

How did you go about getting it started?

I thought, "Hey, why not ask people to donate their old shoes? Depending on their condition, these shoes can be cleaned and then be donated directly to a sponsoring/partnering organization." We held our first shoe drive at my school, Turner Fenton Secondary School, and the support was tremendous - we collected about 100 pairs of shoes in a week!

Who is your project benefiting, and how?

Our project is mainly benefiting those in our community who need these resources the most - people who aren't in the financial position to be able to go out and purchase new footwear at shoe stores. It is also benefitting us, the volunteers, because it allows us to connect with these people and others in need. In turn, we inspire other young people and adults to become involved in our community.

Magnificent Kids!

Who were the key people that supported you, and how?

The key people that supported me are the *STEP* Executive team and my parents who have been a tremendous help. Also, students of Turner Fenton Secondary School and Macklin Public School and the Bramalea Saint Presbyterian Church congregation have all been great supporters because of their constant guidance and mentorship.

In addition, ACCESS Charity (Allowing Children a Chance at Education) has been a great "big brother/sister" to us, because of the continuing guidance and support they provide. Daniel Francavilla and Aminah Haghigi, the Executive Director and Marketing Manager respectively, have assisted *STEP* in getting on its feet and getting publicized in local newspapers and television shows.

How much financial assistance did you have, and from whom?

We have received donations that amount to $3,000 coming from multiple single donors: Saint Presbyterian Church, ACCESS Charity and United Way of Peel Region. We use this assistance for cleaning equipment, transportation costs and conferences/workshops for Peel youth to get involved. This is actually an area where we would require some help - so if you're interested in donating, please give us a shout!

How will you keep your project going into the future?

The entire *STEP* team hopes to see *STEP* grow and expand in the future. We will continue setting realistic and achievable goals for ourselves, while also trying to expand and get other communities, in the Greater Toronto Area, involved in our movement. Also, we are currently providing footwear to people in our community - but it would also be rewarding for us to be able to have a more global impact by being able to transport shoes to developing countries across the world.

How have your peers responded to you setting up the project, and do they (or can they) get involved in any way?

My peers have been extremely supportive in setting up *Shoes To End Poverty*. The *STEP* Executive Team, which consists of Vithuran Sukumar, Yash Sachar, Amn Marwaha, and Pratik Parmar have helped in creating the online presence, financial base and organizational structure for *STEP*.

As a group, we have also worked together in establishing partnerships with other charities such as ACCESS charity and we continue to hold biweekly meetings to discuss how to advance our mission and goals. Other peers, such as the students of Macklin Public School, were also inspired and out of the goodness of their hearts, chose to collect more than 150 pairs of shoes for our organization. So, yes, the constant support of school peers and other friends is a fantastic motivator and encourages me to keep going with my project.

Do you see yourself as ordinary or extraordinary?

I see myself as an ordinary person striving to attain something extraordinary. I'm very much like anyone else my age - a video game and television-loving, sports-obsessed high school teen. But in addition to that, I strive to set myself apart by engaging in meaningful community service, which serves as a reminder to other students that being young most certainly is not a barrier to reaching their full potential, both for themselves personally and in service to other people.

What is the most important thing to you?

The most important thing to me is making the most of life. I sincerely believe in constantly learning more about the world and how we, as youth, can best meet the needs of people around us.

Magnificent Kids!

What are your strengths?

I believe that my strengths include integrity and a compassionate spirit. These characteristics really help me in bonding with people on a personal level and being able to reach out to others with whom I have never had any prior contact (i.e. online outreach to other students).

What are your weaknesses?

One of my weaknesses is that I expect perfection from myself when completing a task, which often results in my having to continuously be wary over seemingly insignificant errors. I regard these problems as flaws in myself and this kind of approach really becomes counterproductive over time. That being said, I am trying to learn how to use this to my advantage by reducing the amount of repeated mistakes and by thinking critically and analytically about my decisions and their consequences.

Does your project require you to focus on your strengths?

My project absolutely requires me to focus on my strengths. In social service, being able to authentically feel for the suffering that someone is going through, allows one to understand exactly what needs to be done. For example, understanding that there were people who did not have appropriate footwear, in addition to other amenities, allowed me to understand that shoes would be the start of helping those individuals to change their lives. Although someone else might think that something else would be more beneficial, my compassion allowed me to put myself in that person's shoes and understand what he/she would want - which in this case, was shoes!

Who is your greatest role model and why?

I credit my father with being my greatest role model. My dad immigrated to Canada from India and really struggled during his initial years to make it here. My father has taught me, and continues to teach me, the value of hard work and its relevance to one's success.

Of all the people in the world, who inspires you the most?

Narayanan Krishnan, an Indian social worker, is the person who inspires me the most. He quit his career as a leading chef and began supplying meals to the homeless. In fact, it was Mr. Krishnan's CNN Heroes video, which opened my eyes to the poverty in the world and how it is our obligation to help one another. His selflessness and humility make him an individual who embodies everything I want to become.

How/where/why did you learn to care globally?

A lot of my perspective regarding thinking and caring about the world as a whole comes from my unique educational background. As a student in the International Baccalaureate, a rigorous high school academic programme that stresses the need for globalism and unity among people of different backgrounds, I find myself thinking increasingly about the implications that my community service activities have on a significantly larger scale. In addition, the Internet is an invaluable resource for keeping up-to-date with the laudable things that youth, many of them younger than I, are achieving by getting involved and making a difference.

If you could change one thing in the world, what would it be?

The almost quintessential answer to this question would be that I'd like to see no suffering in our world. But that simply isn't realistic. There is too much suffering in the world for a miracle to happen and make everything disappear. These things probably won't go away in a hundred days, ten years, or probably in our lifetimes. But in the words of John F. Kennedy, "Let us begin". And youth are one of the best ways to make this change happen.

What do you think are the ingredients for success?

I believe in three ingredients for achieving success: passion, ambition, and adaptability, not necessarily in that order. In order to succeed at anything, you have to genuinely want to do it, which is why being passionate about something is a key ingredient. Once you have your passion established, all you have left to do is plan and follow through. A lot of people don't have the ambition to keep on going. I believe that, to a certain extent, our generation is being taught that mediocrity or quitting is acceptable. To succeed, you need to understand how important it is to follow through with your goals, realize when something isn't working out and move on if necessary. Being adaptable is crucial. For example in Grade 8, I had originally chosen engineering as my career, but once I discovered the extent of humanitarian work and philanthropy that one could become involved with, I haven't looked back, and continue to follow through with my passion.

What is your global vision?

My global vision is to help young people see their potential as catalysts for effecting meaningful change.

What would be your message to the world?

If I could convey one message to the world, it would be that community service is a uniting force that brings together people of all religions, colours, races, and cultures and that it is our obligation as brothers and sisters to assist one another during our times of need.

If other kids wanted to start up their own magnificent project, what advice would you give them and what steps would you suggest they take?

I'm actually happy you brought this up! Many of my friends, and other young people I've met, and continue to meet online, have always wondered how is it that I've found my passion and stuck with it. To those reading this I say, nothing is impossible. All that is required is some thinking and ambition. For more clarity, I've developed a simple 4-step process, which may help you in finding out what your "calling" is:

1. Think - What problems are in your community? Is there a certain aspect that impacts your life more than it impacts others? What are you passionate about?

2. Investigate - You've figured out what you want to do. Now what? First, try to find existing opportunities. If there aren't any, create them. Be creative, imaginative, innovative and become a social entrepreneur.

3. Implement - Put your ideas into action. Make partnerships. Learn and grow.

4. Reflect - Think about what you have done. Do you want to continue this? If you have a genuine interest and find excitement in what you're doing, you should keep going and just watch how far you can go.

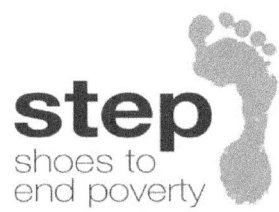

www.shekharkumar.com/step/index.html

"I think the purpose of life is to be useful,
to be responsible, to be honorable,
to be compassionate.
It is, after all, to matter: to count,
to stand for something,
to have made some difference
that you lived at all."
~ Leo C. Rosten

Toby King

Hi, my name is Toby King.

I am 14 years old and I grew up in Australia. I have been at Green School, Bali, Indonesia for three years and have just moved into grade 9. In 2011, I attended a summer camp called Green Supercamp, which is a collaboration between an American organisation, Supercamp and Green School. This is where I learnt about the comfort/learning zone, and many tools that have allowed me to move from my home in Australia and go to a different country and a different life.

I have always been very interested in animals, photography and video. So half a year into my time at Green School, when my dad asked me if I would like to go deep into the jungles of Borneo, Indonesia and make a film about orangutans, it wasn't much of a surprise that I jumped at the chance of a lifetime. We traveled for 45 hours to get to Borneo where I had one of the most amazing experiences of my life: the freeing of a caged animal into the wild. Ever since then, I have been very passionate about creating films that highlight environmental issues and I have created 4 short films.

Magnificent Kids!

Around a year later, for a school project I filmed another movie about the Bali Starling, an endangered bird in Bali. There were close to five left in the wild when Bradley and Debbie Gardner took it upon themselves to save this bird and give it back to Bali. They created a program called the Begawan Foundation. There are now more Bali Starlings in and around Green School than anywhere else in the world.

Another film I finished around four months ago is about Manta rays. I travelled to Nusa Lembongan, an island near Bali where Manta rays are most seen, and interviewed and talked with the people who are helping these animals. After many attempts to get to the place where you can see them most, as the waters were very choppy, I dived and filmed these amazing creatures.

I have just finished working on a new film about the use of chemicals in rice farming and how that affects our bodies and the environment. I completed it in six weeks as opposed to my usual few months that I spend filming and editing.

In October 2013, I was invited to join the Voices of the Future, APEC Youth Council, to participate and film the many Asia Pacific Economic summits that have been taking place in Bali, as well as to meet many of the high level CEOs, Prime Ministers and Presidents of the Asia Pacific region. I was one of 130 youth delegates from the 21 different countries who participate in APEC. They were all 18-24 year olds (I was the youngest one there). We also created a one page declaration that highlighted the issues that youth of APEC believe are important and we presented it to the President of Indonesia, SBY. It was an amazing experience, and one which I probably never would have been able to participate in, if I hadn't moved to Bali.

What does the word 'magnificent' mean to you?

To me, to be magnificent is to be the best you can in any way. Not only to do large, great things but also to do small, great things e.g. a smile could mean the world to someone you don't even know.

What do you give to the world?

I give the world the opportunity to choose to help those who cannot speak for themselves. I try to give them the truth behind those bottles of shampoo that contain palm oil and the fact that by just not buying something or by buying something else, it can help the cause of saving endangered animals.

Why is this important to you?

Whenever I see something that seems profoundly wrong and unjust or inhumane, I try to help those that are not being treated right.

Why did you choose the project/idea that you did?

I don't really know… I just want to be able to make a difference through my passion for photography and film making.

How old were you when you began your project?

I just turned 13 when I filmed my orangutan video.

How did you go about getting it started?

My dad asked me if I would like to go to Borneo to make a film about orangutans and it all started from there.

Who is your project benefiting, and how?

My project benefits those who cannot speak for themselves: orangutans, Bali starlings and Manta rays. It also helps people by raising awareness so they can make choices that are better for themselves, animals and the planet.

Who were the key people that supported you, and how?

My parents supported me to keep going even when it got tough, especially getting through to the orangutans release site, as it was 45 hours one way through jungle and over rivers.

How much financial assistance did you have, and from whom?

I have saved up money, working during all of my holidays, to buy cameras, lenses and other filmmaking gear. My main financial assistance is from my parents. They get me to the places I need to go to film these amazing animals.

How will you keep your project going into the future?

I hope to become a filmmaker when I finish school and focus on documentary and animal or environmental activism.

How have your peers responded to you setting up the project, and do they (or can they) get involved in any way?

As my Bali starling video was a part of a group school project, I had some help with creating it from others in my class.

Do you see yourself as ordinary or extraordinary?

I see myself as an ordinary person in extraordinary circumstances which allow me to travel to the places I need to go to film animals, as well as going to such an amazing school as Green School and being supported by everyone around me.

What is the most important thing to you?

I value going out there and actually doing the things you talk about. I think that no matter where you are or what you do, you can make a difference.

What are your strengths?

My strengths are staying committed and coming up with new film ideas.

What are your weaknesses?

My weaknesses are sticking to the timeline of my films and making sure that I finish and don't spend too much time on the details. When it comes to my filmmaking, I am quite a perfectionist.

Does your project require you to focus on your strengths?

Very much so.

Who is your greatest role model and why?

I don't really know, I have many role models.

Of all the people in the world, who inspires you the most?

In my life I have been inspired by many people. To name a few: H.H. the Dalai Lama whom I met in 2010 when my family went on a trip to India with a group of Tibetan monks, Phillip Bloom, a filmmaker from England who inspires me with the beautiful images he creates, and the many people I have met while making my films:

Magnificent Kids!

educators, animal rights activists, volunteers and the people who just love what they do and care about the future of our planet.

How/where/why did you learn to care globally?

Green School has made me realise that whatever you do, however small or big, has an effect on the people of this world and the creatures that we share it with.

If you could change one thing in the world, what would it be?

I would ask everyone for compassion; I think that if everyone just cared a little bit more, the world would be a kinder and happier place to live in.

What do you think are the ingredients for success?

Integrity – staying true to your values and matching your actions with your values,
Failure leads to success – learning from your mistakes and not letting them get you down,
Speak with good purpose – staying kind with the people around you,
This is it – making the best of every moment in your life,
Commitment - sticking with what you say you will do and following through with your actions,
Ownership – taking ownership of your actions and what you do,
Flexibility – being flexible in your everyday life and really going with the flow,
Balance – making sure you don't spend too much time on certain things and keeping your life in balance.

What is your global vision?

My vision is a sustainable future with light and happiness.

What would be your message to the world?

Try to leave as small a footprint on this earth as you can, as it affects all of us. Practise kindness.

If other kids wanted to start up their own magnificent project, what advice would you give them and what steps would you suggest they take?

I would say, just get out there, do what you can to make the world a happier place, even if it is a small gesture of kindness. Also, stay committed and go with the flow. Many times I have been in situations with my filmmaking where if I had given up I would have regretted it later.

tobykingvisuals.com

Magnificent Kids!

Like us on Facebook to **WIN** your child a $3,000 scholarship to this life-changing programme

www.facebook.com/GreenSuperCampAustralia

Author's final word

"I am only one, but still I am one. I cannot do everything but still I can do something; and because I cannot do everything, I will not refuse to do the something I can do."
~ Edward Everett Hale

I hope you enjoyed reading these captivating stories. By now you will know that anything we want to achieve we can, and you don't have to be a millionaire or a rocket scientist to make change. You will have noticed that everyone in this book is enthusiastic about their project and really know what they are passionate about. They also 'like' themselves and are true to who they are and what they believe in. These things are so important.

Too often, we don't even know what we are passionate about, and our beliefs about barriers in our lives often hold us back. We need to ask ourselves how we can turn our barriers into stepping stones. They might be huge stepping stones and we may have to really stretch our steps and trust they will support us, but ultimately they will not fail us if we believe.

Daniel is an amazing example of how we can turn our passions into something extraordinary and create change regardless of barriers. Daniel has so many obstacles to negotiate every single day, but because he is so passionate about saving the orangutans and their habitat, these obstacles seem almost insignificant to him.

Young Jessica began her life as a tiny, vulnerable soul completely alone and without love, in conditions few of us could ever understand let alone even imagine. Despite this, she has the heart to extend her hand and love to children who are feeling vulnerable and scared; helping create a kinder world.

Magnificent Kids!

Avalon and Dani have autism, and for many this is an enormous barrier, yet they have forged a road of steel with what they are most passionate about. Max lost his dear Great Grams but chose to use his loss to make alzheimers more bearable for others. Jack was also motivated to discover something truly amazing that will potentially save millions of lives because he too lost someone he cared about. Sam, Shekhar, Dallas and Jordyn were all bullied but managed to rise above this and are now doing amazing things.

Each of the stories in this book were written by young people who have chosen to do the best they can with what they have, to make the world a better place. We all have some barriers that could cause us to give up, but ultimately we were all born with a purpose and an amazing capacity to create profound change. So it's time to let go of what we think we can't do, and embrace all of those awesome things we know we can do.

I hope you are now inspired to start creating your own magnificent projects and start shining your brilliant light on this planet. I applaud each and every one of you in advance for starting with that one little step towards creating a better world. Thank you!

Love and blessings,
Kerryn

Special Note to Parents and Teachers

"Children are likely to live up to what you believe of them."
~ Lady Bird Johnson

If you are reading this, you clearly get it! You know that kids need to have their own sets of values that are unique to them, and that being 'mini me' versions of us just won't lead to them feeling fulfilled or magnificent.

You also know we need to recognise what our children are passionate about, and that if they are encouraged and supported to pursue their specific and individualised interests, they will create absolute magic.

For many years I have worked with young people who have not shown any drive for success, and who have become somewhat disengaged and even destructive towards themselves, the people around them and their environment. In some cases they have even been aggressively oppositional at the mere suggestion of hope for future prospects. I have long been on a quest to understand why some sink into despair while others remain so hopeful. Surprisingly, there have also been some people who have switched paths overnight. These things have perplexed me for some time.

'Magnificent Kids!' was inspired by both this perplexity and my own unrelenting belief that we are all innately magnificent and personally responsible for our own failures, successes and journeys.
When I began writing this book, I wondered what types of role models these magnificent kids had in their lives, and how much influence these role models have had in moulding these superheroes. I set about asking the parents a series of questions, hoping to find some theme or quantifiable measure. What I found was the

confirmation that 'you are only as good as your greatest role model'. These parents are superb role models, and we all have what it takes to be superb.

> **Role model:**
> 'a person whose behaviour, example or success
> is or can be emulated by others,
> especially by younger people'

The theme I discovered is that for a child to flourish and to express their true magnificence, they need the following:

- A great role model
- To be appreciated and admired
- To feel safe
- To have something to look forward to or work towards
- To be allowed to express their uniqueness
- To feel loved
- To feel a sense of giving or contribution
- To belong
- To be encouraged, not criticised
- To be respected as individuals with their own unique value systems
- To be supported in what they are passionate about
- To feel they are valuable
- To feel they are doing the best they can
- Opportunities to learn new things to stimulate their minds and imaginations, and to challenge their beliefs

What struck me most about the answers from the parents was how much they admired their children and how positively they spoke about them, and that by having their own global visions they are laying the foundations for their children to think and care beyond themselves.

Here are their responses related to admiration and global vision...

Special Note To Parents & Teachers

What do you admire most about your child?

Deborah Urbach (Alec Urbach)

To settle on one thing that I admire most about Alec would be to limit that admiration. I admire Alec's mind - the mind of an investigator and scholar - he loves to learn because he finds inherent value in the practice. I admire Alec's kindness - there is nothing he won't do for a friend or colleague if it's in his power to do it. I admire his extraordinary work ethic and can-do attitude, and I have yet to see a challenge that Alec hasn't met. I admire his spirit - because he has that rare quality of quiet acceptance while being a roaring force for change.

Lilian Smith (Alyssa Deraco)

Her love for others and her giving heart.

Deborah Theisen (Avalon Theisen)

The list of what I admire about Avalon is very long! She is honest, sweet and cuddly. Seriously, she gives the best hugs in the world. She has strong convictions, even when her beliefs are not popular. When she sees injustice, she has a strong reaction that you can see on her face. She can get lost in pure, creative whimsy. She is not afraid to create. When she says she will do something, she does it. She treats people respectfully. She makes posters about human rights, animal rights, GLBT rights, environmental rights, you name it…and she does them on her own, based on what she researches and believes. She acts on what she feels and believes, doesn't just sit back and do nothing. I love that she enjoys clothes shopping at a thrift shop. I think it is admirable she has asked for "no gifts" at birthdays, or for charitable donations from those who really wanted to share of themselves. For holidays, her list always includes meaningful small things (fabric swatch, bumper sticker with a good message, a used pillowcase to create something new). I love that she is unique and has helped me see the world in wonderful new ways.

Magnificent Kids!

Jim & Lauren Ries (Carter and Olivia Ries)

Dad:
OMG, that is a hard question to answer. As any parent, we are always proud of what they accomplish, especially when their hearts are in the right place. What Olivia and Carter have accomplished is so far beyond my wildest expectations. I admire their sense of commitment and their willingness to share their passion with the world.

Mom:
<u>Olivia</u> – Olivia is very passionate and painfully honest. Sometimes too honest! She knows what is right and she is not afraid to stand up for what she believes in and also has no fear about informing those around her. She does not waiver in her beliefs and stays true to her friends and other important relationships in her life. She values family, friends and life. She believes that no one has the right to take anything's life no matter how big or small... even if you are a spider or a cockroach you have a purpose and a right to life. Olivia always has fun, and enjoys life. She has an incredible personality. She can be very goofy one minute, and "in your face" the next if you are there to threaten her passion or beliefs. She will be an amazing adult and she already is an astounding person! She is determined to make a difference in the world. I have no doubt that she will!

<u>Carter</u> – Carter is very sensitive and caring. He has a big heart. He is always aware of people around him who are less fortunate than he is, and takes extra steps to include them, befriend them, help them feel important, and help them fit in and feel comfortable no matter where we are or who he is with. He constantly keeps the feelings of others in mind before his own needs or wants, no matter how much he will sacrifice, he will continually put others first. He is very passionate and like Olivia he is very honest, however he is more tactful in his approach and I respect that. Carter is remarkably talented in everything he does. He is extremely bright, incredibly artistic in music and in drawing, a natural athlete and he is an exceptional visionary. He has the ability to see beyond what is being presented to him. When he comes across an issue, he has already thought of what the possible solution could be, and in his mind, he has already taken steps to invent this solution.

Special Note To Parents & Teachers

Janet and Ralph Hogan (Clover Hogan)

Janet: Her integrity - When Clover believes in something she is prepared to make sacrifices and stick to them, even if it causes tension with her peer group. For instance, it was when we were still based in Australia, in North Queensland that Clover saw the documentary, Food Inc. and decided the very next day to no longer eat chicken or red meat. Many of her friends gave her a hard time and sent her up about it. It's also much harder sticking to a strict diet in regional Australia, where about the healthiest take away food you can buy is a vegetarian Hungry Jacks burger. Regardless, she stuck it out and 3 years later she hasn't eaten red meat or chicken since. Actually, there was one exception: we took her to France this year and celebrated her dad's 64th birthday at the Tour D'Argent in Paris. The French don't really cater to vegetarians and there was no vegetarian main course, she relented and ate their famous pressed duck dish which I'm happy to say she allowed herself to enjoy, even though I would wager that will be the very last time she lets any kind of meat touch her lips.

Ralph: Firstly as a student and young teen - Clover can never be seduced by the promise of popularity within the herd - into criticising or gossiping about others, but instead defends them. She is a person of great integrity and will not budge on issues of principle. She exercises a great deal of influence on her peers (and her parents!) and is very respected by both her teachers and her peers. She generally remains cool headed, and perhaps more than anyone I've ever known is very self-actualised. Clover is very much her own person. She displays all the qualities I most admire in another human being; she is brave, loyal, honest, self-motivated, highly principled, creative, a defender of the less fortunate (human or otherwise) intelligent, gentle, compassionate, speaks her mind, and is a very hard worker. She is a glass-half-full person and always seeks out the good in others. I am endlessly fascinated by the way she so effortlessly reconciles her (undoubtedly ultra-hip) ego and need for independence - with great warmth and affection for every member of her immediate and extended family.

Magnificent Kids!

Maggie Jessup (Dallas Jessup)

Dallas is intelligent, curious, compassionate, and driven. That is a powerful combination and she has found a way to use her powers for good. Dallas has a multitude of strengths, character, loyalty, diligence, fairness and generosity, kindness, fortitude, and conviction. Her strength of character shines through in all she does. Having gained a huge amount of celebrity, she never let it go to her head. She stayed constant to the purpose of her goals, to help save girls' lives. Her strength of loyalty shone through as she stood by her friends and family never asking for, wanting, or expecting 'special' treatment. Her strength of diligence is apparent with the success of the 'Just Yell Fire' program and her consistent grades throughout high school and college. Her strength of fairness and generosity are seen in the fact that she makes sure to answer every email and sends DVDs so that girls from all over the world can be a little safer, all with no monetary benefit to herself. Her strength of kindness is obvious when you watch her giving a presentation to an auditorium full of girls with compassion for those who have been victimized and need guidance and understanding. Her strength of fortitude constantly amazes as she travels the world, and keeps up with her school assignments and the needs of her friends and family, never complaining. Her strength of conviction has resulted in 'Just Yell Fire' being one of the most prevalent and successful self-defence programs in the world.

Rodney & Penny Clarke (Daniel and William Clarke)

The most endearing quality we see in our children is their perseverance and passion towards a cause. Their sheer determination to follow through on their dreams of saving the orangutans from extinction has continually inspired us as parents. We have always instilled in our children both a sense of responsibility and to have the value of "always doing the right thing", whatever that situation may be.

Special Note To Parents & Teachers

Patrick Eidemiller & Sandy Vielma (Dani Bowman)

Dani's total fearlessness when it comes to reaching her goals.

Jane & Steven Andraka (Jack Andraka)

We admire Jack's determination and hard work the most. Intelligence is not as important as hard work and persistence.

Kathleen Carscadden (Jessica Carscadden)

Jessica was abandoned after birth by her birth parents due to a facial defect. She went on to spend the first months of her life in a 'dying room' (where babies are placed without care to die) in a Chinese orphanage. She continued to live in an orphanage until she was 5 years old. Five years without parents to tuck her in at night, or kiss a boo boo or even just offer a hug when she was sad. She lived without having a single thing that she could call her own - no doll, no stuffed animal, not even a pair of socks that were hers. It would be easy for a child coming from this situation to be hardened or selfish. She is the opposite. I admire daily how this child of mine has overcome everything that life has thrown at her and come out a shining example of happiness and compassion.

Jeffrey & Krystal Schara (Jordyn Schara)

Her ability to think quickly on her feet and give a speech without rehearsing

Helena Adelstorp (Liva Adelstorp)

She is one of the most beautiful, brave, strong and funny people I know. Beautiful heart, Beautiful humour, Beautiful soul.

Magnificent Kids!

Claudia Esau (Louis Robinson)

His ability to communicate with people, his passion and sense of humour

Mary Marete (Luca Berardi)

I really admire his hard work. He really has his goals and dreams in the heart and he doesn't just sit and hope for things to happen, he works hard for them. I also like that he really tries to not leave anyone behind - he is inclusive and allows others to be part of what he is doing. The biggest is that he has a big heart and wants to make the world a better place. I remember him being in a paid gig and donating all of his money to a school in the Mathare slums in Nairobi. When asked why he did it he said that those kids needed that money more than he did, and has over and over again promised me he wants to build them a better school. Having such a big heart at his age is something every parent would love to see in their children.

Linda Wallack (Max Wallack)

His empathy, great work ethic, and desire to help others

Lori Lowinger (Nicholas Lowinger)

I admire Nicholas' determination and degree of empathy for others. I admire that he doesn't see differences in people, but rather their similarities. I admire that he stands up for what he believes in. I admire that he does not follow the crowd if he doesn't agree with what they are thinking, doing or feeling. I admire that he wants to change the world and is determined to do so.

Nadine Bouler (Olivia Bouler)

I admire her ability to speak from the heart. Her passion for the environment is so sincere that people couldn't help but listen.

Special Note To Parents & Teachers

Ken and Jennifer Wright (Olivia Wright)

Definitely her passion and big heart for others. She can talk to anyone - one on one or in a group of 250. She knows no fear when it comes to sharing H.U.G.S. and her other volunteer projects with others.

Chas Lam (Sam Lam)

What I admire most about Samuel is his work ethic. He rarely gave up on challenges, both mental and physical as exemplified by his never-give-up attitude on his project, tennis and academics. Rarely do I see him give up a goal that he had set for himself. He has a solid plan and he works hard to achieve his goal steadily with determination.

Parvinder Kumar (Shekhar Kumar)

The thing that I admire the most in Shekhar is his great sense of humour, his social skills and the fact that he possesses wisdom and maturity far beyond his years.

Sono King (Toby King)

His kindness, his calm, confidence with a lack of arrogance, how considerate of others he is, his tenacity and ability to stay focused... I could go on and on... It is my privilege to share this journey with him.

> "Raise your children to love and embrace others.
> Tell them they are beautiful;
> they may grow up to be stars one day,
> and "beautiful" will never mean as much in a magazine
> as it will coming from you."
> ~ Kaiden Blake

Magnificent Kids!

What is your global vision?

Deborah Urbach (Alec Urbach)

One that includes a peaceful, healthy, and entrepreneurial environment for each generation. If we keep our eye on innovation and education and hold respect for the arts and humanities, people will hopefully be too busy creating and practicing their humanity to cause too much trouble.

Lilian Smith (Alyssa Deraco)

My vision is to help as many kids as we can and to someday be able to travel to other countries and meet the kids that we help.

Deborah Theisen (Avalon Theisen)

My global vision is human rights in practice for everyone and that every person will feel respected as being a meaningful, appreciated part of our world.

Jim & Lauren Ries (Carter and Olivia Ries)

Dad: Since learning about the issue of plastic pollution and seeing first-hand the effects on our environment and all the animals, I would have to say that we want to try and teach everyone around the world that we all need to realize what we are doing to our earth, not just now, but for generations to come. I want to help Olivia and Carter spread the word and teach more kids how they too can be the solution to the issue of plastic pollution and to continue to lead by example that we all need to be compassionate about all living things.
Mom: I am more of an animal lover than a people lover. It breaks my heart how some cultures have little regard for animals and I often find I am in immense conflict with embracing humanity and my deep love for innocent beings. In an ideal world I would love to see every culture respecting all beings, and living side by side in peace where there is limited fear and suffering.

Special Note To Parents & Teachers

Janet and Ralph Hogan (Clover Hogan)

Janet: I believe we are currently undergoing a kind of spiritual metamorphosis which will involve a complete redefining of all of our values (particularly in the west.) When the dust has settled, I see a world where everyone understands that we are not individual operators each vying for the biggest piece of the pie. That we are in fact one giant, interrelated, interdependent organism called humanity. It is only through intense cooperation, not competition, that we have any hope of ensuring our continued survival on this planet.

Ralph: That the unprecedented burgeoning of spiritual/moral/metaphysical awareness throughout Western Civilisation gathers sufficient momentum - and in time - to short-circuit the otherwise inevitable destruction of our planet from the exponential explosion of middle-class appetites across all those continents we once called third world.

Maggie Jessup (Dallas Jessup)

Peace and kindness. What a world this would be if people made decisions with others in mind. You don't have to become Mother Teresa, but if whatever you do is with the mindset of improving the world around you, this world would be a much kinder place. Bias, bigotry, greed and elitism don't have a place in society. Eliminating those traits would be a great start to improving the world. The only way we know to do this is through education and fairness.

Rodney & Penny Clarke (Daniel and William Clarke)

Simply, as parents. our vision is to support our children in whatever it is they want to do in their lives.

Magnificent Kids!

Patrick Eidemiller & Sandy Vielma (Dani Bowman)

Dani is in a unique position to make a significant impact on the lives of others with Autism around the world. So many parents are so overwhelmed with the day to day effort that it takes to make it thought the day with all of the challenges of autism that they don't have a chance to look out into the future to leverage the special obsessions that many with autism have. With Dani, her love of animation and storytelling really was the key to reaching into her world and bringing her out into the family and community. Her work in peer mentoring and teaching has made a significant impact on her own confidence, social skills and ability to lead others that will be important for her to be successful professionally. We hope that her experience will motivate and inspire others to follow their dreams as well.

Jane & Steven Andraka (Jack Andraka)

We would like every kid to be able to have a good education and learn how to contribute to the world.

Kathleen Carscadden (Jessica Carscadden)

I've never really considered myself to have a global vision. I'm just a mom of two amazing kids. Our family values volunteer opportunities that can be done as a family. We are blessed that my husband works for a local laser manufacturer, Cymer, that provides many volunteer and community service opportunities. We are a family of very limited means, we don't own a home, we drive old cars and we are aware, every day, that there are those who have less. So we do what we can to help, and I think that seeking to find a way to do good every day has influenced and encouraged Jessica to begin her project... seeking to bless others with stuffed animals she no longer needed or loved.

Jeffrey & Krystal Schara (Jordyn Schara)

If all teens were required to either create or just volunteer with a community service project, then perhaps there would be more empathy in our world.

Helena Adelstorp (Liva Adelstorp)

I hope more and more of us wake up and find the heart to live a more sustainable life and in harmony with nature.

Claudia Esau (Louis Robinson)

That all individuals would act in an ethical and authentic manner and accept their responsibility in creating a safer, greener and more compassionate world.

Mary Marete (Luca Berardi)

I think my view of the world is that if we loved our neighbour as family, then we would do all the best to make their lives better. Being humble and loving others for who they are not what they have.

Linda Wallack (Max Wallack)

More cooperation between individuals and countries

Lori Lowinger (Nicholas Lowinger)

I am hopeful that the world will be at peace and that there will be equality for all.

Magnificent Kids!

Nadine Bouler (Olivia Bouler)

Climate change is on the horizon. It will take many voices to make the full-scale global changes required to save the world as we know it.

Ken and Jennifer Wright (Olivia Wright)

To see H.U.G.S. carry shoes to every country! For Olivia to be able to hand deliver shoes around the world and to help her carry out her dream of building an orphanage.

Chas Lam (Sam Lam)

My global vision is human rights and dignity. Treating people with different cultures and languages as your family members. It is a very hard thing for human beings to do as we have seen numerous wars and conflicts in our history, but I believe with good education humans can treat each other with respect and love each other more.

Parvinder Kumar (Shekhar Kumar)

My global vision is quite similar to Shekhar's - helping young people recognize the limitless power for change that they possess which not only impacts our cities, states/provinces, or countries, but rather, the world as a whole.

Sono King (Toby King)

My vision for this world is that kindness, forgiveness and emotional intelligence will prevail and transform our world from the inside out. I see this happening in so many simple places already. May it continue to flower. My vision is that humanity (including myself) become more and more aware of the consequences of their actions and that they make the effort to change, in all areas of looking after ourselves, our communities and this magnificent planet we live on.

Special Note To Parents & Teachers

By now I imagine you're thinking that these parents are no different from you, and they're not. They are supportive, nurturing, respectful and they fully acknowledge what is important to their child. They admire rather than criticise their child and they are not afraid to express their love and praise. They have their own global visions, and they understand how important it is for their child to also have a global vision that is unique to themselves. By sharing our visions with our children, they too become interested in global issues and are more likely to contribute to a better world.

As you read the stories you will have noted that two of the superheroes, Avalon Theisen and Dani Bowman are on the Autism Spectrum. The number of people being diagnosed with autism is rising dramatically and it is still a mystery as to why. It is common for parents to feel shattered when their child is diagnosed with autism, in fact any form of real or perceived disability, as there is a lot of grief and loss associated with the feeling that 'my child will never grow up to have a normal life'.

I asked Avalon's mother, Deborah Theisen, to contribute to this section as I believed it to be vitally important for every parent and teacher to understand the difficulties, but more importantly, how the right kinds of support can lead to extraordinary outcomes.

Here is Deborah's response...

What is your key philosophy in raising children?

Avalon is our only child, so we have a family of 3 humans (many more including the animals that share our home). I have never been asked this question, but in thinking about my key philosophy to raising children, I would have to say the willingness to pay attention, be flexible and make changes.

When Avalon was an infant, we had a crash course that no book could prepare us for, much like most parents, I suspect. Of course, I was conditioned by my own upbringing and previous experiences with children, but the reality of raising a child has so many dimensions. I quickly learned than even a young baby is a very unique individual, with very specific preferences and needs that need to be respected.

We had a bouncy chair, musical swing, all kinds of things that Avalon wanted nothing to do with. What she did enjoy was being in a sling (my kangaroo baby!) or simply staring up in the sky at the trees and clouds above her. If only we had waited to see what she preferred, we could have saved a lot of money and effort with all those other things!

As preschool years approached, we knew we wanted to homeschool. Complete with a rigid pre-packaged, private school curriculum that I had done very well within as a child, I was so excited to set up Avalon's school area. Though some parts went alright, I was quickly in for a surprise that things overall were not going so well. Once I learned to take a look at how Avalon learned best, and not impose how I learned best on her, we made changes and she blossomed.

One thing we have learned more about over the years is allowing Avalon to be part of decisions about herself... not just making choices for her because she is the child and we say so. What that looked like at age 2 months, 6 years and now is different, of course. Over the years, we have all grown. We will continue to grow, sometimes making mistakes. Essentially, we are her parents, but it is her life, and she has to be free to be who she is.

As parents, we have learned to listen more to Avalon and respect her personal beliefs, goals and being. We know that as she grows, she will transition more to her own separate path, even if it is still linked closely to ours. She has to have confidence in her beliefs, her actions and choices, not trust something only because I say so, for example. She has a great mind, heart and soul. Many times she has led us on her journey. Our family has made many changes because of her, from the food we eat to the cars we drive. By listening to Avalon and by trusting her, our lives are richer.

Special Note To Parents & Teachers

There are many stories like this, but they all add up to the willingness to change and do what feels right. What worked for me as a child may very well not work with Avalon. What works today may not work tomorrow. At the end of the day, guiding Avalon as she grows and matures is a great honour, and we want to respect her, as well as the process.

Deborah

While autism does have its share of obstacles, it is really important to remember that these kids just see life a little differently and so process things differently. They may find it difficult to express themselves and often people will disregard or belittle what they are wishing to express simply because their communication style is different. Temple Grandin beautifully states that autistic people are 'different, not less'.

I am overwhelmed with emotion as I write this because it matters so much to me that people with autism and any other disability or disorder are seen for their *a*bilities. I believe that it is our responsibility to ensure that *everybody* is given the opportunity to show the world the unique gifts they have to offer.

Daniel Clarke is a case in point. Although Daniel is predominantly confined to a wheelchair due to cerebral palsy, this has not stopped him showing the world his remarkable capacity. He is saving lives and nothing is more significant than that. Given the opportunity and support, a person with a disability can show us a world of possibilities that we never imagined.

"It's our choices that show what we really are, far more than our abilities."
~ J.K. Rowling

Magnificent Kids!

There is another angle. When kids want to do amazing things, there may be some kids who want to tear the confident kids down. Dallas Jessup who created 'Just Yell Fire' saw this first hand. Her mother Maggie wrote to me hoping I would, in some way, express her thoughts in the book. I think she says it better than I could, so here's her letter...

Dear Kerryn,

If this book is geared towards kids wanting to get involved it is important to note that Dallas has had her share of jealousy at high school. There are those, as in any high school, that taunted her and belittled her because of what she has chosen to do – 'Just Yell Fire'. She has been featured in many magazines, radio, TV, newspapers, and even books. Through it all, she never lost sight of the big picture. She is forgiving and has been able to use perspective to not let it all affect her, or slow her down. I admire this, she was the youngest in her class, but has shown great strength and character not seen in most adults.

College was a totally different experience. Her peers at Vanderbilt were accomplished in their own right, so her peer support and the admiration of others on campus grew tremendously. She was celebrated and accepted, school mates went out of their way to help her, compliment her, meet her and promote 'Just Yell Fire'. It is amazing what a couple of years of maturity and education can accomplish. So, it is important to know that pushback and jealousy are going to be a part of this process for a very short time, but once you get past this, the world opens up and others are able to see what you see. This makes all the difference in the world.

Warmest regards, Maggie

I hope that sharing these insights from parents has given you some encouragement and the opportunity to recognise that if your kids want to start something amazing... they can, and you are not alone. Now it's your turn to release the bright star that has been dormant within your magnificent kids and help them discover a stage and set design uniquely crafted for their passions.

What's your cause?

Here are a few ideas to help you get started with your own magnificent project. Hopefully, as you work your way through these sections, you will become aware of what it is that really moves you to action. You first need to know what you are passionate about, because passion keeps your heart in the project and it keeps you energised and focused. Once you know what you are passionate about, you will be able to match that passion to a cause and start contributing and making changes that are unique to you.

> "Don't ask yourself what the world needs.
> Ask yourself what makes you come alive,
> and go and do that.
> Because what the world needs is
> more people who have come alive."
> ~ Howard Thurman

What's that 'thing' that gets you excited?

So what *is* that thing? Maybe there are a few things. Think about things that you love doing or that you are really good at. What hobbies and interests do you have that when you are involved in them, time simply passes without you noticing? What's that 'thing' you do because you love it? It is important not to dismiss any passions that might come up for you because you think they are not directly related to making a better world.

I have a friend who loves push bike racing, and recently she told me that she felt this passion had no way of contributing to a better world. I suggested she could host a bike-a-thon, complete a ride across a great distance, or even facilitate bike maintenance workshops to raise money for a cause. The actor, Samuel Johnson

Magnificent Kids!

recently rode a unicycle around Australia to raise awareness for breast cancer and in the process raised over 1 million dollars. He called it 'Love Your Sister' and was inspired by his own sister's battle with cancer.

What if you love computers but just can't see how computers could help? Easy! You could set up a project that helps get computers into the classrooms of poorer villages in countries like Fiji. Or you could design a company that develops free or discounted websites for non-profit organisations. Perhaps you could make mini movies to educate students about bullying. You might be absolutely hooked on photography. Great! You could sell beautiful photos that reflect the brighter side of your cause and use the money to create change, or alternatively you could take photos of problem issues and present them to the world to help educate people and raise awareness. My dear friend Jo-Anne McArthur has done just that with the dark secrets of animal use and abuse. Her book 'We Animals' tells the true story, but her presentation of the photos is more thought provoking than anger instigating. She is creating a huge ripple for animal rights by using her passion for photography. Always believe that what you are personally passionate about can make a big difference, and will mean the world to those you are setting out to help.

Notes...

Which cause are you passionate about?

Ask yourself 'What happens in the world that really upsets me?' What is that 'thing' that really tears your heart out when you read or hear about it, or even see it with your own eyes? If the answer is something like people hurting animals, then your cause might be animal rights, justice, equality or welfare. This might also extend to human rights. Or you might get upset about people littering or wasting water, so your cause might be to do with the environment or pollution. Perhaps it breaks your heart to see kids dying from starvation, or when disaster strikes an area, you wish you could rush straight there to help. Your cause might then be disaster relief or poverty. Alternatively you could ask yourself, 'What absolutely makes my heart sing?' Some examples might be orphaned children being adopted, stranded animals being rescued from natural disasters, hospitals in poor communities resourcing vital equipment, stray dogs being vaccinated or desexed, schools being built in third world countries, or women in patriotic communities becoming empowered. Your cause will be something that stirs up strong reactions in you. Listen to your heart... it knows the answers!

Notes...

Magnificent Kids!

What would be your message to the world?

If you are still a little unsure about what you are passionate about or what your cause is, imagine you are standing on a big stage in front of thousands of people. Imagine you are not nervous because you truly believe in your message and making a difference in the world, and more importantly, everybody gathered in front of you is really interested in what you have to say. Imagine that your message had the potential to make history and would be significant in bringing about a better world. Now, imagine (really imagine) yourself confidently delivering this message.

- Did you feel powerful and that nothing could stop you?
- Did you notice that when you are sure about something, and when it comes from your heart, people believe in you and are prepared to follow you?
- Did you notice how authentic you felt?

This is how it feels to be genuinely in the flow with your purpose. Nothing can stop you!

Notes...

The million dollar question

If you had one million dollars to make the world a better place, what would you spend it on?

Notes...

Hopefully these questions have helped you become clearer about what your 'thing' is. Setting up a project may seem a little overwhelming, but it doesn't have to be. It really depends on the size of the project you intend to set up. If you want to start a non-profit organisation that will have global reaches and have a huge impact on the world, then yes you will have to work a little harder. But the reward will be just as big. On the other hand, if you want to make a difference without all the fuss, there are many things you can do, on a much smaller scale, that can have a huge impact on the lives you directly touch.

When we pick up a pebble and throw it into a pond, we no longer have the pebble. It has left our hand and we are now unable to control its ripple. But imagine if one of your 'pebbles' was talking to a group of friends about the plight of starving kids in Africa. Perhaps your friends appear indifferent to your concerns but without you knowing, one friend goes home and talks about what you said with her family over dinner. The friend's younger brother sitting at the dinner table becomes so touched by the conversation that he starts to ask WHY? He is so driven by his WHY that his life and academic choices soon lead him to become an International Aid worker. He spends the next 15 years travelling to and from Africa and in this time manages to set up sustainable produce gardens in hundreds of villages. Now, how important is every little pebble we drop into a pond?

Project ideas to get you thinking

- Make up some pamphlets about something you care about
- Volunteer at a dog shelter
- Promote products that are not tested on animals
- Make recycled gifts
- Hold an art or photography exhibition related to an issue
- Promote one day of the week as a healthy food day
- Host a charity party and ask your friends to bring a donation
- Do a presentation about an issue
- Start a petition
- Have your classroom exhibit a series of causes
- Donate clothes or toys to a homeless shelter
- Facilitate a 'solutions' brainstorming session
- Hold a fundraiser showing a film about a cause
- Hold a debate at school about an issue
- Start a survey about awareness of an issue
- Create a film clip or movie about your cause

Don't think you have to do million dollar things to make change. Often the smallest things make the biggest differences. One thing is for sure... there is nothing more satisfying than reaching out your hand to reduce the suffering of another.

Break it down

It is impossible to have a gigantic dream and think it will happen overnight. It won't. Even worse, if you think it will happen overnight and it doesn't, you may feel like a failure. That's not what we want. The key is to break it down into achievable steps. There might be 5 steps or there might be 100. Keep the steps manageable so that you have successes at each stage. This will keep you motivated and you will gain strength and momentum with every success, and eventually your gigantic dream just might become possible.

Action Plan

An action plan is a template for you to write down the steps you need to take to get your project up and running. As you fill it in you will see that the steps don't seem as far out of reach as you thought.

Action Plan - Donate clothing and toys to a homeless shelter

What do we need to do?	How do we do it? (Steps)	Who is responsible?	When do we need it done by?
Make a list of local homeless shelters	Look through the local telephone directory	Susie	5/3/2014
	Do an internet search	David	5/3/2014
	Ask parents and teachers if they know of any	Susie, David, Alison & Michael	5/3/2014
	Decide which shelter to donate to	Susie, David, Alison & Michael	10/3/2014
Advertise your proposal and include a drop off point and pick up date	Create fliers	David	15/3/2014
	Hang fliers up in shops and around school	Susie	18/3/2014
	Do a letter box pamphlet drop	Michael	18/3/2014
	Announce at school assembly	Alison	20/3/2014
Collect donations	Organise parents as drivers	Susie, David, Alison & Michael	5/4/2014
Deliver donations to homeless shelter	With parents as drivers	Susie, David, Alison & Michael	5/4/2014
Advise of the outcome	Create notices of thanks and outcome	David	8/4/2014
	Hang notices up around school and shops	Susie & Michael	10/4/2014
	Announce at school assembly	Alison	13/4/2014

Magnificent Kids!

Mind Map

Some people find an action plan a bit too structured and prefer to think in pictures or diagrams. A mind map is a way of drawing all the main components of your project and seeing the details of each part.

You can also use a mind map to fine tune your cause. For example if you're really passionate about helping children you can identify some key areas and then choose one to start working on. In our action plan we chose homeless children, so on a mind map it would look something like this...

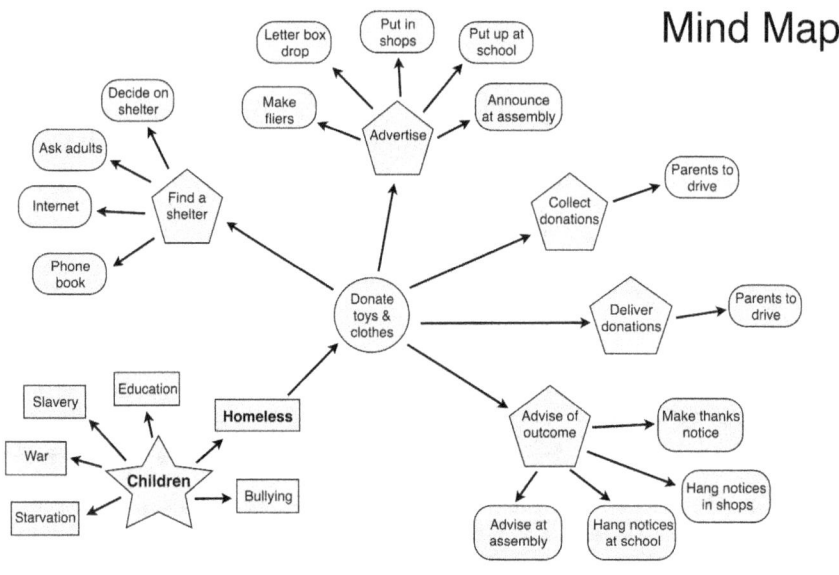

Hopefully these ideas have helped you find your passion and cause, and you're now inspired to get started with your own magnificent project. Remember that each of us has an amazing capacity to make change, and that we all have our own unique gifts, talents and strengths that enable us to be a superhero.

Good luck with your magnificent project!

What's Your Cause?

Action Plan - Donate clothing and toys to a homeless shelter

What do we need to do?	How do we do it? (Steps)	Who is responsible?	When do we need it done by?
Make a list of local homeless shelters	Look through the local telephone directory	Susie	5/3/2014
	Do an internet search	David	5/3/2014
	Ask parents and teachers if they know of any	Susie, David, Alison & Michael	5/3/2014
	Decide which shelter to donate to	Susie, David, Alison & Michael	10/3/2014
Advertise your proposal and include a drop off point and pick up date	Create fliers	David	15/3/2014
	Hang fliers up in shops and around school	Susie	18/3/2014
	Do a letter box pamphlet drop	Michael	18/3/2014
	Announce at school assembly	Alison	20/3/2014
Collect donations	Organise parents as drivers	Susie, David, Alison & Michael	5/4/2014
Deliver donations to homeless shelter	With parents as drivers	Susie, David, Alison & Michael	5/4/2014
Advise of the outcome	Create notices of thanks and outcome	David	8/4/2014
	Hang notices up around school and shops	Susie & Michael	10/4/2014
	Announce at school assembly	Alison	13/4/2014

Magnificent Kids!

Mind Map

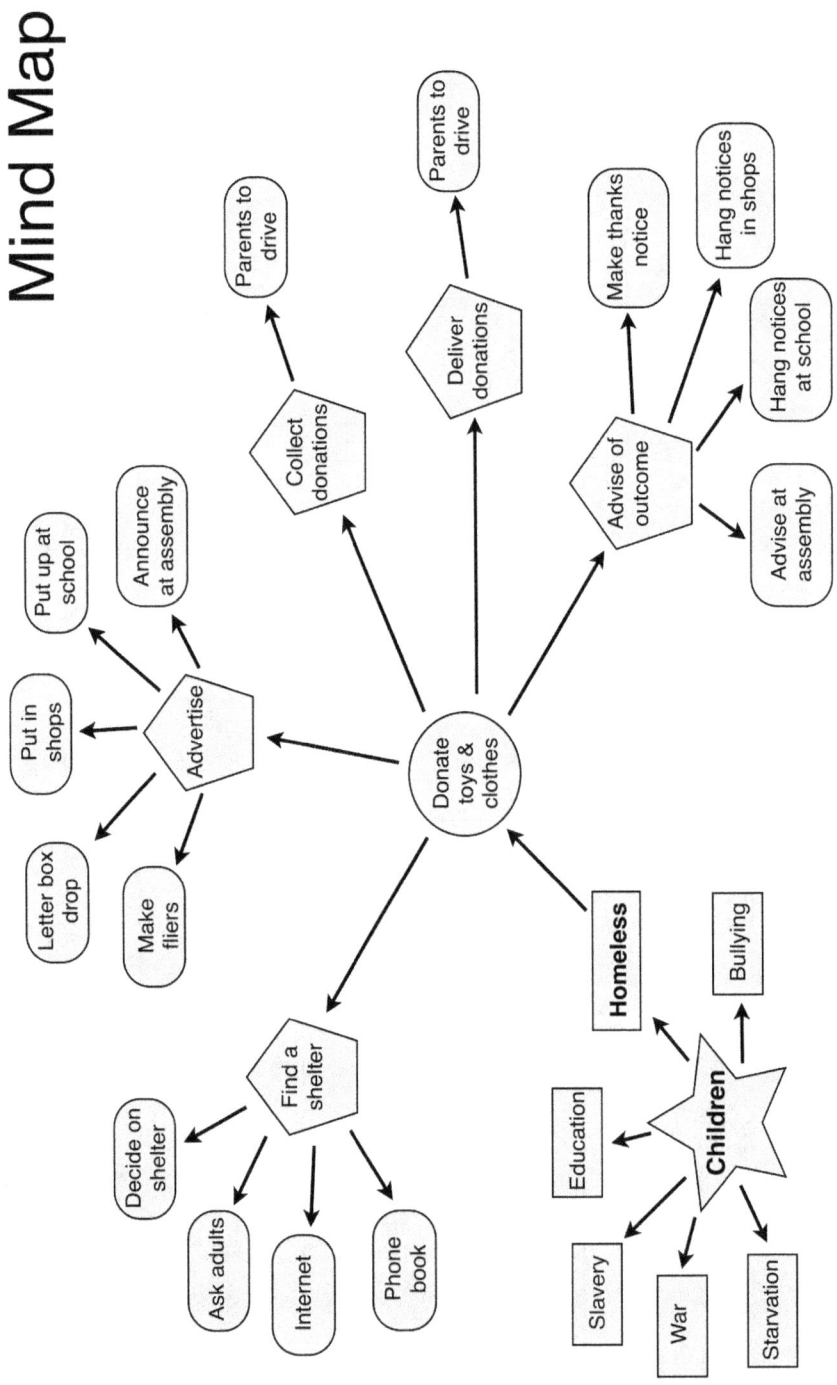

About the Author

Kerryn Vaughan grew up in a small, country town in Australia - but without limitation, she learned to speak in many universal languages. For years, Kerryn has used her passionate voice for all types of human justice, animal rights, social equality and the environment at large. Beyond her long-time dedication of philanthropy and humanitarianism, Kerryn is also an accomplished singer-songwriter with an array of worldwide visibility on many animal welfare websites - many of her songs are written and themed to support animal rights in all capacities. Kerryn holds great notoriety in the animal community - she is well respected for inspiring people to advocate and take responsibility (and accountability) for their choices and how it will reflectively impact our society - ensuring the safety, protection and adoption process with dignity for all animals, while absolutely free of cruelty - on every level.

Kerryn is also an educator with an amazing capacity to transform lives. She specializes in disability, autism, behaviour and personal development - but has taught many subjects both in Australia and overseas. With highly effective results, Kerryn has guided adult learners through their darkest days - mentoring them to a purposeful life of value and self-worth, while foreseeing a positive future with clarity. In addition, Kerryn has spent many years working with disengaged youth - helping them to find their inner-spark and motivation for life.

As Kerryn has received numerous awards and qualifications for her good works - she dismisses these types of accolades and recognition as mere 'pieces of paper' that do not accurately reflect her true impact or intentions regarding charity and contribution. In Kerryn's own words, 'The real evidence of my achievements is sitting in three drawers full of emails, cards and personal letters from people whose lives I've touched - in one way or another, with my energy bestowed upon them through compassion and true faith in every one of them.'

Years ago, Kerryn's greatest revelation in life came when she lost her sister to cancer. It was then when her vision about her life's purpose and mission were most vivid. Today, Kerryn is a living testimony of how time is really precious for all of us and how life must not be taken for granted, at any given moment. Kerryn is a modern pioneer who leads by example. She shares her gifts of wisdom and knowledge, life skills, acquired talents and her many selfless acts for the sake of others. It's no wonder Kerryn's life mantra states, 'If we can make a difference, why wouldn't we?'

It is a great privilege to be associated with such an extraordinary person like Kerryn Vaughan. For years, I've known her to be that rare gem in any society - the one who cares more, helps more and gives more - the one who puts her words into action, while doing it with a compassionate and selfless heart. With the utmost confidence, I know that *'Magnificent Kids!'* will not only inspire communities near and far, but will also help us to rediscover and redefine the real essence of all humanity, all seen and expressed through the simplistic eyes of an insightful child - simply brilliant! I value Kerryn as the epitome of good character and true integrity, and her remarkable book is a milestone!

Scott Katsura – *International Recording Artist & Author of "I'm Writing My Own Story – A Kid's Guide To Becoming An Extraordinary Person"*

Copyrights and Credits

Copyrights

Magnificent Kids - © Kerryn Vaughan

Stories and answers:
Alec Urbach - © Alec Urbach
Alyssa Deraco - © Alyssa Deraco
Avalon Theisen - © Avalon Theisen
Carter & Olivia Ries - © Carter & Olivia Ries
Clover Hogan - © Clover Hogan
Dallas Jessup - © Dallas Jessup
Dani Bowman - © Dani Bowman
Daniel & William Clarke - © Daniel & William Clarke
Jack Andraka - © Jack Andraka
Jessica Carscadden - © Jessica Carscadden
Jordyn Schara - © Jordyn Schara
Liva Adelstorp - © Liva Adelstorp
Louis Robinson - © Louis Robinson
Luca Berardi - © Luca Berardi
Max Wallack - © Max Wallack
Nicholas Lowinger - © Nicholas Lowinger
Olivia Bouler - © Olivia Bouler
Olivia Wright - © Olivia Wright
Samuel Lam - © Samuel Lam
Shekhar Kumar - © Shekhar Kumar
Toby King - © Toby King

Photos:
Alec Urbach - © Alec Urbach
Alyssa Deraco - © Alyssa's Bedtime Stories
Avalon Theisen - © Conserve It Forward
Carter & Olivia Ries - © One More Generation
Clover Hogan - © Clover Hogan
Dallas Jessup - © Just Yell Fire

Dani Bowman - © Dani Bowman
Daniel & William Clarke - © CTQ Management Consulting Pty Limited trading as Tears In The Jungle
Jack Andraka - © Jack Andraka
Jessica Carscadden - © We Care Bears
Jordyn Schara - © Jordyn Schara
Liva Adelstorp - © Liva Adelstorp
Louis Robinson - © Louis Robinson
Luca Berardi - © Y.A.R.H
Max Wallack - © Max Wallack
Nicholas Lowinger - © Gotta Have Sole Foundation
Olivia Bouler - © Olivia Bouler
Olivia Wright - © Olivia Wright
Samuel Lam - © Samuel Lam
Shekhar Kumar - © Shekhar Kumar
Toby King - © Toby King

Cover photo - Avalon Theisen - © Conserve It Forward

Sketches:
Alec Urbach, Alyssa Deraco, Carter & Olivia Ries, Clover Hogan, Dallas Jessup, Daniel & William Clarke, Jack Andraka, Jessica Carscadden, Liva Adelstorp, Louis Robinson, Luca Berardi, Olivia Wright, Samuel Lam, Shekhar Kumar & Toby King - © Kerryn Vaughan
Avalon Theisen - Frog © Avalon Theisen
Dani Bowman - Anime © Dani Bowman
Luca Berardi - Y.A.R.H plan © Luca Berardi
Max Wallack - Brain © Max Wallack
Olivia Bouler - Bird © Olivia Bouler

Logos:
Alec Urbach - © Alec's Animated Schoolhouse
Alyssa Deraco - © Alyssa's Bedtime Stories
Avalon Theisen - © Conserve It Forward
Carter & Olivia Ries - © One More Generation
Clover Hogan - © Bali Animal Welfare Association
Dallas Jessup - © Just Yell Fire
Dani Bowman - © Powerlight Studios

Daniel & William Clarke - © CTQ Management Consulting Pty Limited trading as Tears In The Jungle
Jack Andraka - © Jack Andraka
Jessica Carscadden - © We Care Bears
Jordyn Schara - © Wisconsin Prescription Pill and Drug Disposal
Luca Berardi - © Y.A.R.H
Max Wallack - © Puzzles To Remember
Nicholas Lowinger - © Gotta Have Sole Foundation
Olivia Bouler - © Olivia's Birds
Olivia Wright - © Tennessee H.U.G.S.
Samuel Lam - © End To Cyber Bullying
Shekhar Kumar - © Shoes To End Poverty
Toby King - © Toby King Visuals

What's your cause? - © Kerryn Vaughan

Quotes:
As credited with individual quotes.

Credits

Cover Design: James William - New York / USA

Sketches - David Simpson: for Alec Urbach, Alyssa Deraco, Carter & Olivia Ries, Clover Hogan, Dallas Jessup, Daniel & William Clarke, Jack Andraka, Jessica Carscadden, Liva Adelstorp, Louis Robinson, Luca Berardi, Olivia Wright, Samuel Lam, Shekhar Kumar & Toby King.

Editing & Proof reading - Maggie Griffin

www.ingramcontent.com/pod-product-compliance
Lightning Source LLC
Chambersburg PA
CBHW071900290426
44110CB00013B/1219